# *My* Autism HatRack

# *The Life Flip*

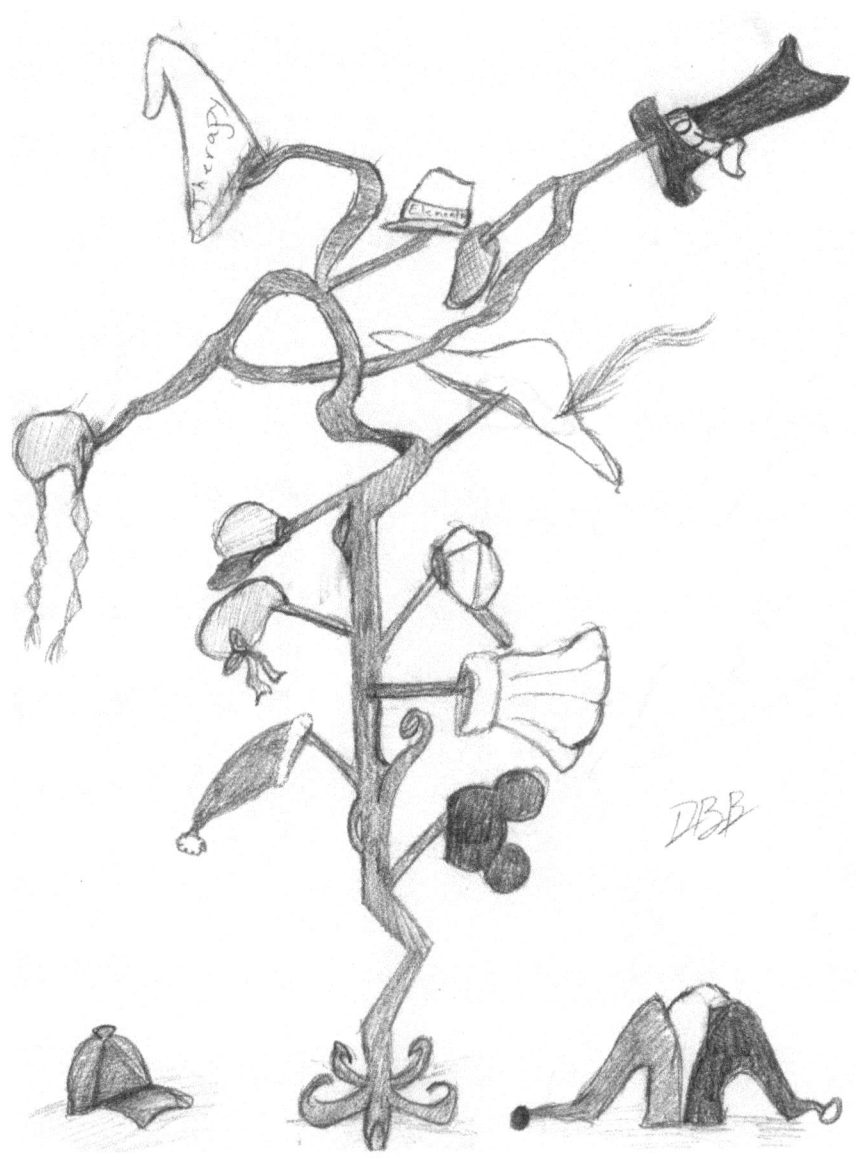

*Original Artwork by: Danielle Brice Bordelon*

**For more "Hats", workshop information and online videos go to:**

**www.MyAutismHatRack.com**

# My Autism HatRack

## *The Life Flip*

Hope and Healing in the World of Autism,
One "Hat" at a time.

### Maureen Brice Bordelon

Advocate, Author & Mama

My Autism HatRack Publishing
Copyright © 2013

Copyright© 2013 by Maureen Brice Bordelon

All rights reserved.

No part of this book may be used or reproduced by any means, graphic, electronic, or mechanical including photocopying, recording, taping or by any information storage retrieval system without permission in writing from the publisher.

This book is intended as a resource and guide to provide a summary of autism research, experiences, treatments and therapies. None of the information presented in this book is meant to be a prescription for any kind of treatment, medical or otherwise. References to any organizations and/or materials within this book are for convenience only and not intended for endorsement. No therapy should be initiated unless recommended and supervised by a qualified professional. The medical professional and the parent or guardian of the child needing treatment are responsible for weighing the risks before beginning any of the therapies, medical or alternative treatments described in this book. The author and publisher are not responsible for the misuse of information provided.

The author of this book does not dispense medical advice or prescribe the use of any technique as a form of treatment for physical or medical problems without the advice of a physician, either directly or indirectly. The intent of the author is only to offer information of a general nature to help you in your quest for emotional and spiritual well-being. In the event that you use any of the information in this book for yourself or loved ones, which is your constitutional right, the author and the publisher assume no responsibility for your actions. Some names have been altered or adapted to conceal the identity of certain people or parties within this book. All opinions of the author are hers alone and do not reflect the opinions of any other family members or Organizations. The author and publisher are neither liable nor responsible to any person or entity for any loss, damage, or injury caused or alleged to be caused by the information in this book.

Second Printing 2013
ISBN 978-0-578-13073-6

Published by My Autism HatRack Publishing
www.MyAutismHatRack.com

Library of Congress Cataloging-in-Publication Data
A CIP Catalog record for this book is available from the Library of Congress
   Bordelon, Maureen Brice
   My Autism HatRack – The Life Flip: Hope and healing in the world of autism, one "hat" at a time/ Maureen Brice Bordelon
   Includes inspirational quotes (trade paper)

Photography by David Bordelon, Gregory Bordelon and Maureen Brice Bordelon.
All photos published in this book are the property of Maureen Brice Bordelon
Original Artwork by Danielle Brice Bordelon

*This book is dedicated to my amazing family:*

*David, Gregory, Danielle and Jonathan*


*And to all the families raising beautiful, unique children who experience the "life flip" each day.*

# CONTENTS

GRATITUDE… ..............................................................................xi
WELCOME TO MY AUTISM HATRACK.........................................xiii

**PART I - *THE LIFE FLIP*** ...............................................................1
CHAPTER 1:   THE GOOD LUCK KISS OFF .....................................3
CHAPTER 2:   WHACK! WELCOME TO AUTISM! .........................13
CHAPTER 3:   HELLO GOD, ARE YOU THERE? IT'S ME MAUREEN........19
CHAPTER 4:   WHEN A DOOR CLOSES, A WINDOW OPENS .................27
CHAPTER 5:   ….AND THEN THE THERAPIES ................................33
CHAPTER 6:   FINDING MY "HOPE HAT" ....................................45
CHAPTER 7:   GRAB A BOWL AND MAKE YOUR "LIFE MIX"...........51
CHAPTER 8:   BREAKING IN MY "ADVOCACY HAT/HELMET" ..............63
CHAPTER 9:   THE "SIBLING MIX" ..............................................75
CHAPTER 10: THE SCHOOL ADVENTURES ...................................81
CHAPTER 11: GOD WASN'T SILENT ANYMORE...........................87
CHAPTER 12: THE HEALING .....................................................101
CHAPTER 13: THE MISSING PIECE OF THE PUZZLE .....................105
CHAPTER 14: MY AUTISM OUTLOOK .......................................117

**PART II - *MY "HATS"*** ..............................................................121
CHAPTER 15: THE "MAMA HAT" .............................................125
CHAPTER 16: THE "PMS HAT" .................................................127
CHAPTER 17: THE "IMMUNOLOGIST HAT" ................................131

Chapter 18: The "What Diet Now? Hat" ......................................135

Chapter 19: The "Essential Oils and Autism Hat" ...................139

Chapter 20: The "Wonder Mama Headband" ...........................143

Chapter 21: My "Hope, Dream, Believe Hat" ...........................147

Therapies on My Autism HatRack ..............................................151

Spiritual References ...................................................................155

Treatment References ................................................................155

Notes ...........................................................................................157

*GRATITUDE...*

I am grateful to Jonathan for having patience and love for me as his Mama, while he teaches me how to see the world through his eyes. I am thankful to David, Gregory, and Danielle for their love and support as I travel my divine pathway and our journeys are intertwined. I love you all.

I believe in Heaven and Earth Angels that come in and out of our lives as we need them and lean on their wings for help and support. I have been blessed to have many angels in my life that have been compassionate during times of need and celebration:

*Mother Mary, Tessa F., Blaine C., My Parents Bob and Susan and Brice Family, My Bordelon Family, Mimi, Don, The Divas: Laura, LaLa and Carolyn; Dina G., Danette G., Betsy W., Jennifer K., Kim S., Liz S., Amie W., Nathalie M., and all the amazing Warrior Parents who have shared their beautiful children and lives with me.*

I believe God plans out the Universe for us to experience our journey, while gifting us free will to make our choices along the way...**Choose wisely and make every moment count.**

# Welcome to My Autism HatRack

*The Month of April is the official World Autism Awareness Month. In our home, the effects and characteristics of Autism have been an "awareness" 24 hours/7 days a week for 12 years and counting. The awareness of Autism has grown along with the number of families who are dealing with the pain, mystery, finances, and exhaustion of this epidemic. The journey is for the strong of heart and faith wrapped up in Teflon armor; these remarkable participants of Autism do not volunteer for this journey, but are drafted into the depths of an altered path of unknown certainties and enormous barriers. It is no wonder that the Autism Community is made of warrior parents and children that strive for answers, treatments, acceptance, hope, and compassion.*

*I am a member of this community and have nurtured my child, family and myself through heartache, confusion, loss, joy, hope and enlightenment. Along the way I have had to wear different "Hats" in numerous fields of interest to attain goals, treatments and remedies, all of which I have accumulated and are hung on:*

## My Autism HatRack

*Follow me on my journey of finding strength, hope and healing where I create and use My Autism HatRack every day –*

**Get ready to put your "Hats" on!**

*Blessings & Stay Strong,*

*Maureen*

# PART I

## *The Life Flip*

CHAPTER 1

## THE "GOOD LUCK" KISS OFF

*"It is during our darkest moments that we must
focus to see the light."*
- ARISTOLE ONASSIS

I had finally gotten into a comfortable position after hours of flopping around in my sheets when I felt a warm sensation between my legs, and realized that I had wet the bed. My first thought was, holy crap, how did that happen? Then I remembered and reached over to my husband, David, and said, "Honey, wake up. My water just broke. The baby is coming."

Jonathan Robert Bordelon made his debut at 7:33 am, on a beautiful August morning in the year 2000 after 5 pushes (yes, thank you very much!). He was a perfect, healthy baby brother to his 2 siblings: Gregory (6) and Danielle (18 months). Jonathan came into the world with wise, old-soul eyes that instantly told me this kid was going to change the world. How he has done that is a story still in the making, but the journey so far has been one of perseverance, heartache and faith.

David and I were living in Amarillo, Texas, when Jonathan was born and trying to get back to our native Dallas. We had both taken jobs with a computer company in 1998 that was making new strides with e-commerce and cutting-edge technology. We were working 10-12 hour days when in the spring of 2000, we discovered the company was mismanaged by the owner and unethical things were happening. One morning we walked into the office to find staff members had been fired over the weekend and investment funds missing. Seeing the e-commerce ship sinking, David and I resolved to break ties with the company, which spun our lives into a "Life Flip". We went from 2 kids, a dual income, a house, 2 cars, private Catholic school, and a nanny; to no income, 3 kids, and minimal job opportunities. We needed to move back to Dallas for work and sell our house. Harmony was replaced pretty fast with stress, worry and fear.

We had our house on the market for 8 months and realtors were calling with an hour's notice, so most days after having the baby, I would race around trying to clean up after 5 people, 3 of whom were less than 3 feet tall. The magic day of selling the house came when a realtor had scheduled a showing next door and the clients saw our FOR SALE sign. They knocked on the door and asked to see the house. "No, problem", I thought. The house was clean enough and all I had to do was grab the kids and make a hasty exit out the back door. I asked the realtor to give me 5 minutes and then come on in the house.

I called out to Gregory, who was in his room playing with his Thomas the Tank Engine train set, to get in the car and then went to scoop up Danielle (26 months), and Jonathan (8 months). That was when I smelled it. The most horrendous smell emitting from our youngest child. Jonathan had landed one of his "toxic bombs" and there was no way I could diffuse the fumes. I heard the back door open and David walked in making perfect timing and asked, "What is that smell?"

"Jonathan" I replied as I kept moving the kids towards the back door. "A realtor and buyers are outside waiting to come in and we need to evacuate now." I grabbed a diaper bag and all 3 kids while David was double-checking the rooms for any embarrassing debris. We piled our toxic-fumed family into the car and drove down the block so I could flip open the back of the SUV and change Jonathan's crap-filled diaper, before we all passed out.

That event is so clear to me as a shift change in our lives. First, we sold the house to the couple that walked into our foul fumes, but obviously smelled past it and saw the beauty of the home.

The second thing was Jonathan's polluted dump. It had been an ongoing occurrence through the months and I had even talked to his pediatrician about it. The pediatrician had suggested changing from regular baby formula to soy formula, thinking Jonathan may be lactose intolerant, but other than that, she dismissed it as a normal occurrence. My Mama gut was saying otherwise. His bowel movements were like nuclear bombs that radiated crap I couldn't even describe. Looking back at this moment, I wish I had been more knowledgeable about GI issues in babies. I wish I had someone say to me:

*"WARNING!!! You are so right Maureen- this is not normal. Your baby's gastrointestinal (GI) tract is screwed up and you need to know his immune system is under attack."*

All I knew at the time was our perfect, healthy baby was getting sick a lot, had colic, toxic poops, contracted whooping cough at 3 months, ear infections, then was dosed with antibiotics. He had been on schedule with all his immunizations so; I didn't understand why he was so unhealthy…until a few years later.

We sold the house in Amarillo to the spontaneous couple without having to fumigate, and headed back to the Dallas area. We landed in a suburb north of Dallas, and I was feeling the "Life Flip" turning. David got his old job back, Gregory was getting settled into grade school and Danielle, Jonathan and I were maintaining our daily routine of PBS, limited viewing of stoned out tellie tubbies, and macaroni art. For the first time in 15 years, I was officially a stay-at-home Mom. My board meetings were about making cookies and choosing the best learning strategies to teach our kids. The "Life Flip" of the past year was starting to flip back around…I was so wrong.

Despite Jonathan's colic and toxic poops, he was a happy and active baby. He went from crawling at 10 months to walking for a week then running and balancing on the backside of the couch. I was envisioning gymnastics for him and future Olympic gold medals.

When I would watch him line things up, I thought it was thoughtful of him to keep his toys all lined up and out of Mama's way. When he started lining up videos, shoes and house plants, I started to think maybe he didn't care about Mama's clean house, but more his obsessive structure.

Jonathan had a great giggle. It was one of the infectious giggles you hear and even though you have no idea what the funny punch line was, you would start to laugh. Jonathan would do this spontaneous giggle through out the day while he was sitting on the floor with his back to the TV, or playing with a set of teething keys and out of the blue, start giggling.

Well, then I would start giggling, then Danielle, then Gregory and David until we were all laughing at the happy sounds from Jonathan but all being clueless as to the joke.

When Jonathan wasn't giggling however, he could break into a shriek pitch of pain so fast, I would be running to him thinking he had cut off a limb or another kid was sitting on top of him. When I would reach him, he would be in the middle of the floor, lying over a ball or couch cushion and I would have no clue as to the source of pain.

Months would go on with the pattern of giggles and shrieks and by the time Jonathan was 13 months old, something was seriously wrong with him. He was sick with ear infections, croup, hives, constant runny nose, reflux, vomiting, and diarrhea. He was a non-verbal, inattentive little boy who reflected no recognition of his surroundings, dangers, or even his siblings.

We went to get his hearing tested at around 15 months old because I thought he was deaf and couldn't hear me call his name. The doctor said his hearing was fine, so it was the neurological and biomedical issues that I had no clue how to address and my Mama intuition was screaming warning bells!

The "Life Flip" was about to do more than just a flip, it was revving up for a life spin into another dimension of chaos. Through the next few months of inconsolable screams, stomach aches, reflux, hives, eczema, ear infections, sinus infections, antibiotic treatments, irrational behaviors, lack of eye contact…I knew something was wrong with our baby and the doctors were blowing it off.

I wanted to go back to our old Pediatrician in Dallas, where we had the kids as patients since Gregory was born. At first, they had us on a 7-month waiting list as new patients, but after contacting the doctor directly through voice mail, we were put on the 3-month waiting list as pre-existing paychecks. It was the Fall of 2001, and since David and I were still working off one car, I wanted to consolidate my efforts by taking all 3 kids to the pediatrician for their well check visits.

The nurse was going over the checklist of milestones for each child, when she asked me, "So Jonathan is 16 months, right?"

"Yes", was the answer I managed to utter as I caught Jonathan mid-air when he jumped off the exam table almost landing on his sister. Gregory was stripped down in his underwear, running in a circle with the tissue-sheet from the exam table loosely tied around his neck, flying behind him like a cape.

"Hi Miss Nurse, I'm Captain Underpants!" Gregory proudly stated, posing as his favorite cartoon book character, with his hands on his hips, bare chest puffed up, as if he were ready to conquer any mishap headed his way.

The Nurse glanced at Gregory and her face softened with a small smile and then she looked at the "checklist" again.

"How many words does Jonathan have in his vocabulary?" She asked me. I remember holding Jonathan on my lap as he was squirming to get down and run in circles. I started to mentally count his words: 1- he says "Gego-eee", 2- "Dan-yell", sounds and grunts...

While I was still counting on one hand Jonathan's verbal skills, the nurse's voice interrupted my thoughts, "200?" she asked, because she was tired of waiting for my exhausted brain to spout out an easy number.

"200?" I asked shocked. "Uh, no. You can take a couple of zeros off of that number." As I said the words I could feel my heart plummet. 200 words? I knew Jonathan was slow to talk, and he was rambunctious, energetic, didn't listen to me all the time, but why did I never pay attention to how many words he should be saying by now. It wasn't like I was a new Mom and I hadn't been through this before; it was my 3rd time gearing up for the terrible twos.

The Nurse glanced up from her paper work and looked at me for what seemed like the first time and then she looked around the room at my children and sighed. She picked up her clipboard and got up from her stool and said, "Dr. Mayberry will be right in." And "poof" she was gone.

"Mama, I don't think that Nurse knows who Captain Underpants is. That is probably why she wasn't very friendly." Gregory said as he came over to me and hugged my neck.

Everything was going in slow motion. I started to recall all the red flags I had felt about Jonathan, but every time I asked the doctor in Amarillo or spoke with other Moms, I was always told:

*"He's a boy, boys are late bloomers."*

*"He's your third child and their siblings always talk for them so they are "late talkers."*

*"Kids get whooping-cough, yes, even at 3 months and don't worry about the rashes, they will go away."*

*"Antibiotics are safe for any baby and he needs it for his ear infections and whooping cough."*

*"Jonathan has colic and a lactose intolerance. Feed him Soy formula and stop breast-feeding because your diet might be making him sensitive."*

*"Kid's attention spans are so short, don't worry if he isn't coming to his name, he is just busy with other distractions..."*

*"Don't worry about eye contact. Small children have a hard time focusing on things and seeing colors."*

There was a soft knock on the exam room door that brought me back to reality and in walked Dr. Mayberry. He was smiling and he had kind eyes that looked at me with so much concern. I immediately knew Jonathan's accomplishment of knowing 2 words was not hitting a "milestone".

"How are my patients doing?" he asked looking around the room at all three kids.

"Hi Dr. Mayberry, I'm not Gregory, I'm Captain Underpants! But this is still Danielle, my helper, and my little brother Jonathan."

"Well, Captain Underpants, how are you feeling?" Dr. Mayberry proceeded to do physical exams on Gregory checking ears, throat, eyes and then moving on to Danielle, who politely extracted her boo (pacifier) to comply with the tongue compressor check. He moved over to me because I had finally gotten Jonathan back on my lap and still for an ear, nose, throat and chest check.

"Everything looks good Mom. Do you have any questions?"

I was stunned. I thought for sure Dr. Mayberry was going to tell me Jonathan's progress on his milestones was way behind schedule, but he didn't.

I wanted to reply, "No, no questions at all." If I didn't ask if Jonathan was "off" or "behind", he couldn't answer "yes". This was my way out of hearing terrible, life altering news. This was my chance to ignore the red flags that had already been cleared by the doctors. Jonathan might still have a hearing problem and that was why he didn't look at me all the time. Jonathan is just very energetic and his siblings talk for him. We can keep doing sign language because he knows more sign language words then the stupid verbal checklist said he should know….I took a deep breath and said,

"Yes. One question, what is wrong with Jonathan?"

Dr. Mayberry looked at me with his now sad, blue eyes and answered, "Well, I can't be sure, but he does show strong signs of being autistic."

BOOM! There it was. Crap. I should have kept my big, problem-solving mouth shut.

He continued talking, "You need to take him to another Pediatrician named Dr. Hami, but the signs are there."

Signs, what freaking signs? The signs I have been asking doctors and friends about for months; rashes, diarrhea, behaviors, lack of verbiage, eye contact, but was told I was being paranoid and over protective?

I found my voice and asked him, "How do you fix autism? What the hell is autism? Is he going to die? Does autism kill children? Does that mean he is brain-damaged?" I was shooting out questions like bullets, "Why do I have to go to a different Pediatrician?"

Dr. Mayberry smiled sympathetically as he ignored my questions and said, "You need to prepare yourself that Jonathan may never talk or communicate. He will not play and interact with others. You need to prepare yourself that he may need to be in an institution when he is older." Now he was the one throwing bullets and bombs at my heart, each one more injurious than the last. What the hell was he talking about? My 16-month-old son was not going to be put into an institution!

"Dr. Hami is a Developmental Pediatrician in the area who sees kids on the Autism Spectrum. I can't really do anything for Jonathan but here is her number." He reached into his pocket and to my surprise, he had Dr. Hami's number already written on a card and handed it to me. Well shit. Kind, blue- eyed, bomb throwing Dr. Mayberry already had his kiss-off, exit strategy planned out. He stood up and politely shook my hand and said, "Good luck and don't forget to go next door and get the kids' vaccinations up to date."

I was numb. Did he just shake my hand and say "Good Luck". Yep, he did. Dr. Mayberry walked out of the exam room leaving me with life-altering news, Captain Underpants running in circles in his tissue-cape, Jonathan grabbing at Danielle trying to swipe her boo out of her mouth and the room filled with GOOD LUCK. I think about that moment often and wonder if the doctors have any idea how insensitive their words are, leaving parents to feel so hopeless with the news of autism and words like, "Good Luck".

I was pulled from my numb state with Danielle's shriek of "No baby!" at Jonathan's swiping of her boo, Gregory crumpling up his tissue cape and I gathered my beautiful little blessings and walked out to the checkout desk. The office manager told me to go next door to get the kids' immunizations up to date and I actually looked at her and said, "Dr. Mayberry just told me Jonathan has autism (even as I said the words out loud it didn't seem real), should I wait to do anything with him until we see the other Pediatrician?"

She looked at me like I was nuts and said, "Immunizations have nothing to do with autism and they are safe, so you need to update the kids. That will be $60.00 today and you can pay next door for the immunizations." I pulled out my checkbook and was waiting for her to say "good luck" to me too, but she didn't. She just gave me my receipt and turned around.

Trusting our children's pediatrician, I dutifully did as I was instructed to do, and I updated our children's vaccines minutes after being told Jonathan had autism. I didn't know enough about autism and the connection toxic vaccines had to our children's biological defenses. In the 20 minutes it took for me get our kids shot up with toxic shit in the guise of immunizations, (unwittingly doing even more damage to Jonathan's immune system), I called David and told him to come get the kids and me from the doctor's office. I didn't put together the whooping cough all 3 kids got after their DTaP vaccinations in 2000, the terrible diarrhea and gut issues Jonathan suffered from in his short life, the numerous hives and rashes that the doctor in Amarillo suggested were sensitivities and just to change soaps and detergents, but the rashes never got better.

Yep, none of those things were thoughts in my mind. The only thing I was trying to wrap my brain around was "autism" and as I waited in the parking lot for David, holding Jonathan on one hip, Danielle in the stroller and Gregory hugging my waist feeling my sadness and hopelessness…I cried. Not the big, hysterical, ugly boohoo cry, because that came later; but I stood there with silent, heartbreaking tears rolling down my face and hitting the parking lot concrete and thinking how much I will always hate the words:

"GOOD LUCK"

CHAPTER 2

## WHACK! WELCOME TO AUTISM!
## THE SPINNING WORLD OF:
## NO RULES, NO GUIDELINES AND NO GUARANTEES!

*"Do not go where the path may lead, go instead where there is no path and leave a trail."*
- RALPH WALDO EMERSON

Our "Life Flip" had just taken another somersault and left me numb. I felt more alone in that moment than any other in my life. Jonathan had severe autism. We had a diagnosis, but not a treatment plan and I felt like I had been given a death sentence for our 16-month-old baby. His future was robbed by a disease I couldn't cure or heal according, to Dr. Mayberry. Hell, I couldn't even get an answer as to what it was or understand where it come from.

I had fear of the unknown and I was terrified. I was mad at the unjust of it all and I was upset at myself. Why? How could this happen to our baby? Wasn't I doing all the things I was supposed to? Jonathan was actually our first child I kept on schedule with vaccinations and doctor visits, so why was he sick? I was following all the damn rules of life. What did I do wrong that gave our son autism? Why?

Silence. That was my answer, and that was when I felt God and my relationship drift. We had so many "Life Flips" happen in the past two years, I felt that I was flying the plane alone and God had packed his parachute and ejected somewhere far, far away.

I felt vulnerable with things out of control and I didn't like uncertainty. The first thing autism takes away from you is control. I could not control what I didn't understand. I could not control ailments effecting Jonathan because he had limited verbal skills and could not tell us where or what his pain was. That, to me, was the hardest aspect about autism. It doesn't attack you directly, it targets your child and makes you watch and feel your baby's pain.

Autism robs your child from your grasp and transports them into a world of confusion, pain, fog and isolation. It starts chipping away at your whole family by taking away the control you think you have as a mother protecting your children. You learn fast, that the world can be a very judgmental, scary, non-accommodating place for you and your child with "extra needs".

I hated autism and I wanted to heal our baby. I was 35 and I knew a lot of people, but none of our friends had a child with autism. The only reference I had about autism was the movie <u>Rain Man</u> and trying to imagine our 16-month-old baby as Dustin Hoffman counting cards in Vegas was not relatable to me at all.

So my "problem-solving mind" started at the beginning. How did Jonathan get autism? Was it in our family's genetics? I was combing through the 100+ people from my Irish side of the family and I just couldn't think of anyone having autism. David's side of the family was much smaller, but no autism that we knew about.

I was clueless to the cause in 2001, and obviously, so was the medical field because no one knew how to treat it or isolate the cause. I remember going to the computer at home and pulling up AOL and typing in AUTISM. The computer didn't recognize the word. It was redlined and kept trying to change the word search to ARTISTIC.

There were no articles of research I could find. Nothing. Silence...until I heard my son's shriek from the other room signaling yet another bout of tummy aches and head banging. I knew I was on my own to heal Jonathan. It would be up to me to find solutions.

I picked up the card my "Good Luck" doctor had given me and called Dr. Hami's office. To my shock, she answered the phone. I was so excited I started talking really fast and crying and talking and crying, and finally I got the coherent words out- "Our son was just diagnosed with autism, can you help me?"

Dr. Hami said, "You need to take a breath." I remember that so well. Her calm voice on the other end of the phone telling me I needed to breathe. I gulped down my blubbering and took a slow, long breath. And it worked.

I was still anxious about getting help, but I was calmer when I asked, "Can I make an appointment and do you take insurance?". I desperately wanted to transport myself through the phone into her office, sit across her desk and suck in all of her knowledge and treatment methods.

"You can make an appointment and my earliest available date is January 10, 2002. I do not take insurance because insurance doesn't cover autism. I charge $350.00 for an evaluation office visit". I thought I heard her wrong because it was September 2001. There is no way I could wait 4 months to see "an expert" to start helping my son. I NEEDED help NOW! No insurance coverage? $350.00- wowza!

My internal thoughts became my "outside voice" and I had vocalized my distress. Dr. Hami was actually very gracious and responded with no-nonsense directions;

"While we are waiting for your appointment date, there are 3 things to look at to treat your son's autism:

1. **Environment** – toxins, chemicals, heavy metals, etc...
2. **Allergies** – You child may suffer from severe allergies so you need to get his allergies tested and adapt his diet.
3. **Genetics** – DNA testing, chromosome disorders, etc..."

This was the most valuable advice I had received in the last few days as a desperate Mama. I had no idea what a lot of the things were. I knew heavy metals were things like steel and iron-right? And genetics was about eye color and X & Y chromosomes-right? And allergies were about seasonal pollen and animal dander-right? Wrong. I was so naive on the biomedical aspects of the ailments assaulting our son's body, I had a lot to learn but I was willing.

A few weeks later, I received a call from Dr. Hami's office informing me that she had closed her offices and moved out-of-town. My first appointment with the only physician (that I knew of) who treated autistic kids just cancelled my son's chances of getting out of the fog.

*Whack! - Welcome to Autism Maureen! The spinning world of: No Rules, No Guidelines and No Guarantees!*

I was pissed off and this emotion was becoming the norm. I had finally gotten a glimmer of hope to get some guidance and help, and WHACK-it was gone! Since, I wasn't one to sit around and wait, I had to start finding solutions. We had no extra money to find another Developmental Pediatrician at $350.00 an hour, so I looked at allergies. Our insurance would cover going to an Immunologist, so I made an appointment with a Dr. Hernandez and took Jonathan in to figure out if he had allergies.

For the next 3 months, our little boy was tested for 3 allergies per 2-hour visit, 3 times a week to see what his allergies were. This was the most painstaking thing for a toddler and his Mama. We would arrive at the office and Jonathan knew by the second visit that the red, brick building was not a fun place to be. I had to invoke my exceptional skills of negotiating with a toddler. This was so foreign to me because I was a Mama with the guidelines of: Mama Rules = Rules are Rules; no exceptions.

This was not an option with Jonathan. If he didn't want to do something, he would let you and the world know. His reactions went beyond the normal kid tantrum into fits of Tasmanian devil episodes (aka scream-fests) that would wear us both out. These scream-fests could happen anywhere and the results would be a small loss of my hair, bruises or bites on my body, self-inflicted bruises by Jonathan leading to exhaustion. So, I had to learn techniques of negotiation with our youngest son because "Mama Rules" were not a choice.

The allergy testing method was horrible. It was a prick test and Jonathan would get pricked with an "antigen" and we would have to wait in the office for an allergic reaction. I would have his portable DVD player ready with his favorite movies and his books to help distract from the pain. It was at this time I found myself loving *Veggie Tales* and grateful for the humor in their children's videos because if I had to listen to the purple dinosaur or the creepy four adult males singing in a compact car, I was going to help Jonathan pull my hair out.

The results of the tests showed Jonathan was allergic to just about everything. Dairy, casein, soy, wheat, sugar, yeast, animals, dust mites, trees, grass, and more. Of course I hadn't even heard of gluten or casein before, but I had heard of soy because Jonathan had been on soy formula for his entire young life.

When we got home the day we discovered his allergy to soy, I gave Jonathan water instead of soy milk and within 4 hours I got eye contact from our son for the first time in a long time. That is when I knew; diet and biology were going to be our immediate direction.

I started to hang my first hat on My Autism HatRack in that time frame. I call it the "Hard Hat" Construction Helmet. This is where I started construction on the foundation of healing and breaking down the walls of autism that had Jonathan trapped. I wanted our baby to be free of pain, anger, anxiety and "the fog". I wanted to be able to hold and hug him without him squirming away from my touch. **I wanted to hear him say, "I love you Mama"**. I had to construct a place of calm for him to grow and feel safe. I needed to heal our son and I was going to do it.

The "Hard Hat" is my oldest "Hat" from My Autism HatRack. I have worn it every day of Jonathan's life. It's hard "outer layer" protects my head as I crash into multiple treatments, countless therapies, special education administrations, insensitive people in public places, and negative energies to open the door to hopeful endeavors, positive progress, wonderful successes and miracles!

My "Hard Hat" led to many more "Hats" that would eventually hang from My Autism HatRack[1]. Each "Hat" would be worn to help me deal with this journey that included everything from nutrition to Epigenetics. I had to identify our son's allergies, create a diet that would heal not harm him, NAET allergy elimination treatments, biomedical interventions, Essential Oils, occupational therapy, speech therapy, Advocacy, ABA, RDI, EDS therapy, neurofeedback, HBOT, Chelating therapies, Interactive Metronome, Music Therapy, Vision Therapy, GI tests, Neurological evaluations and more…My Autism HatRack was becoming assembled.

---

[1] Part II: See more of My "Hats"

CHAPTER 3

## HELLO GOD, ARE YOU THERE? IT'S ME, MAUREEN.

*"God grant me the serenity to accept the things I cannot change, the courage to change the things I can, and the wisdom to know the difference."*
- REINHOLD NIEBUHR

This point in my journey, I was pretty drained. I prayed to God for answers and direction, but my connection to him was full of distorted crap. I was still angry and sad at the autism curve ball and how unfair it was. I was jealous of my friends and their easy lives with their "non-autistic" kids. We were trying to "blend in" at places like Gymboree for some normal adventures and my friends would all be sitting in the circle with their toddlers in their laps ready to float the gigantic, colorful parachute, while I was chasing Jonathan around the room like a maniac and he was giggling or screaming oblivious to the 20 other kids in the room following their "Mama Rules".

But more than anything, I was heartbroken that our baby was almost 2 years old and didn't even say, "Mama".

I redirected my spiritual focus by praying to my Grandmother Mimi, who had passed away in 1997. Mimi was my super grandmother and the only grandparent I remember having growing up. She lived an amazing life, had 4 kids, 23 grandchildren and when she went to heaven on the eve of her 88th birthday, our family lost our matriarch but gained a heavenly angel with some serious Irish spunk. After Mimi's death, I could still feel her presence in every day occurrences and it gave me comfort. I didn't really know how to explain it without men in straight jackets coming for me, but when I made a decision I had been troubled about, I would hear someone whistling a song she used to whistle or see something that would remind me of her and I would feel her reassurance of my decisions. I started to call these moments "Mimi-isms". I prayed every day for her to give me her maternal strength to deal with another day in the world of autism and the roller coaster ride that wouldn't stop.

I found myself leaning on my guardian angels and earth angels with whom I believed in strongly. Being raised catholic in a family of seven, Church, the Holy Trinity and Mother Mary were a big part of my life. I was the 4$^{th}$ child out of 5, so that consisted of hand me downs, getting your butt to the car when it was time to leave, or you would be left behind, and learning early that if you didn't open your Christmas gifts that were the same shape as the other kids, at the same time, you would never be surprised. Well, I take that back, you could have gotten the orange unisex sweater instead of the bright green one.

I had an older sister and two brothers and then a younger sister that made up a great dynamic of personalities, love, and adventures. We celebrated every holiday big with my Mother decorating the house and making special holiday meals. We had a great network of family friends and would gather for holidays, rosary prayer sessions and special masses said in honor for people in need.

All 5 kids attended a private Catholic school that was adjacent to our church and my Father did his parental, volunteering duty of coaching the basketball teams while my Mother volunteered at the school's Mothers Club. Like every other catholic family attending Christ the King, you had at least 4 or more siblings throughout grades K – 8, so we had a lot of coaches and a lot of moms keeping tabs on us all.

I felt my parents did a great job expanding my religious experiences growing up. Where my religious base and upbringing was the Catholic Church, we had family friends who were Jewish. At the age of 10, I went to a Jewish Summer camp and learned about the Torah, challah bread, and the Sabbath. My biggest impact about this adventure, besides being called a "gentile", was how similar the two religions were. It opened my eyes to how religion was the ritual part of faith and while the world had different organized religions with their own interpretations of the Bible, ceremonies, and worship - the common denominators were God, heaven and the afterlife.

This started my curiosity about religion and faith. As I grew older, I recognized that the world segregated people based on their religion. I started to meet people who were Baptist, Methodist, Presbyterian, Church of Christ, Lutheran…and I thought that we were all connected as people spiritually despite the separation of our religions. I couldn't understand the judgmental attitude of religious organizations with the mind set of "our way is the only way", because it went against what they were preaching = God loves us all. Even at a young age, I felt more comfort in the spiritual point of view of knowing God was an all loving God and that heaven was for everyone, not just a particular few.

My spirituality was tested when my Mother started volunteering at a local Hospital and then later took a full time position there as Director of Volunteers.

The Dallas Hospital my Mother worked at specialized in Cancer patients only. She used to take me down to the Hospital when I was 11 years old and pimped me out as a babysitter for the younger kids at the hospital who had Leukemia so their parents could take a night off. These kids were amazing. I still remember the smiles of Kathleen, Stewart and a little girl named Tessa who was bald, funny and wore pink nail polish. We would play dress up with hospital gowns, run wheelchair races through the halls, order pancakes at night from the hospital cafeteria and play pranks on the nursing staff.

Tessa loved to giggle, and that is what I remember most about her. I don't like to think of the times when I would come visit and she would have had chemotherapy that morning and been vomiting all day. She would get swollen, have huge circles under her sunken eyes after each chemo session and she would be too tired to play, so I would just sit and read to her trying to get her to rest. One day I came to the hospital and Tessa was gone. She had passed away and was in God's hands, free from her pain.

The idea that Tessa was never coming back was hard for me to grasp at 11 years old. This was another time in my life I had to make adaptations to my faith. I couldn't understand why these beautiful kids at the hospital had to suffer so much and then most of them would die.

A few months later I met another patient at the hospital named Blaine and he was officially my first crush. He had the most beautiful brown eyes and dazzling smile. He was diagnosed with Leukemia and had come to the hospital for treatment all the way from Colorado. It was surprising for me to meet another kid my age, who was so sick because Blaine was just like the boys in my class and he should have been in school learning and playing baseball, not hooked up to IVs and having to sleep in a hospital room.

When I would visit him, we would play Atari and Pong video games that a local family had donated to the hospital. We would listen to country music, watch TV and Blaine would tell me about how beautiful his hometown in Colorado was. He would tell me about his Dad who was the local game warden and how they would go on hunting trips all over the mountain ranges. Colorado sounded a world away from Dallas and my concrete city life, and Blaine could describe things so well, I could envision his home of Durango and all the lovely people.

One night, I was in the hospital watching another little girl named Kathleen, while her parents went out for dinner. The phone rang in Kathleen's room and it was Blaine calling from down the hall asking me to come down to his room. Kathleen had fallen asleep, so I went down the hall to Blaine's room and when I walked in, there was another girl sitting with him. She looked to be my age with a short, pixie hair cut that framed her pretty face. Blaine made the introductions, "Hey Mo, this is Laura. Her family is the one that gave us the video games to play with."

"Hi Laura, nice to meet you", I came forward from the door with my hand stretched out to shake hers.

"Hi" was all she said as she shook my hand and then turned to Blaine to talk about some trip their family had gone on together. When they finished talking about the trip, Blaine turned back to me and said,

"I wanted you two to meet each other. You girls are going be to great friends." I just stared at him thinking, are you nuts? We just met, how did he even know we were going to like each other?

I smiled and looked at Laura and replied, "Ok, if you say so Blaine. It was nice to meet you Laura. See you guys later." And then I excused myself to go back to Kathleen's room to check on her.

Later that month, I saw Blaine again at the hospital and he was super excited about going home. We went downstairs to the hospital pharmacy and were sitting on the blue padded benches that lined up against the pharmacy hallway, waiting to fill up his prescription. As we were sitting there, I looked at Blaine and he was very pale and weak.

"Blaine, are you sure you are feeling good enough to travel home?" I asked.

"Yep! My Mom and Dad are taking me home this afternoon." He

replied with a huge grin.

"When will I see you next?" I asked naively, sad to see him go.

Blaine reached over and held my hand, "I don't think you will Mo". His words hit me so hard because all the sudden, I knew why Blaine was going home. He was dying and he didn't want to die at the hospital. He wanted to go home to Durango and be with his loved ones.

I could feel the tears welling up inside me and he squeezed my hand. "Don't be sad. I'm not scared. It's going to be ok." Blaine said comforting me. Can you believe that? Comforting me when he was the one dying. He was so fearless and brave. When he reached over and hugged me, I felt his inner strength and knew it would be the last time I would ever see those beautiful brown eyes and dazzling smile. I didn't want our embrace to end, but what made me let go, was that his heart was happy to be going home.

Blaine died a few weeks later surrounded by his family in his majestic mountains. He was a beautiful earth angel that came into my life and showed me strength and fearlessness. He also gave me an incredible gift - the gift of friendship; his and he was right about Laura. We have been best friends since Blaine introduced us over 35 years ago.

To cope with the pain and actions from the Universe, I made up a scenario at the age of 12, that for some reason, only known to God, Tessa, Blaine, Kathleen all had a mission in life to be earth angels and touch as many lives as they could in their short time here. I knew I was blessed to have met them on their journeys and as my journey continued, I felt them watch over me from heaven and they were happy and pain free.

Now, here I was with my own child whose life was being compromised with health issues and I since I felt my direct help line with God was full of distortion and on hold, I started to lean on my angels and Mimi to help guide me in the right direction to heal Jonathan.

CHAPTER 4

## WHEN A DOOR CLOSES, A WINDOW OPENS.

*"...With autism you better have a crow bar"*
- MAUREEN BRICE BORDELON

I was trying to have a normal life with our two older kids by setting up play dates, joining soccer teams and becoming part of the PTA, but it was so hard trying to engage with other Moms who were complaining that their child wasn't using 4$^{th}$ grade vocabulary words in kindergarten while our son was trying to make 3 word sentences. I found myself having to deal with the seesaw of development with our kids and socializing.

One day I met my neighbor, Jane, at the local park with our accumulated 4 children under the age of 5. She had a daughter Danielle's age and a little boy Jonathan's age so the park was a great place to let the kids run around. Unfortunately, I was doing most of the running. We started at the slides, but then while I was talking with Jane about enrolling our daughters in school, Jonathan went right down the slide and sprinted off towards the street. Did I mention that I am allergic to running? Well, I forgot to tell Jonathan too, and he loved to take off. I would have to snag him before a car would come down the street because he had no concept of danger. This was my socializing with friends. Unless I had Jonathan in his stroller or in a swing, there were no more casual conversations about what was on Oprah or who was the latest neighborhood Mom to get a boob job.

Socializing had taken on a whole new perspective. It was exhausting listening to Jane complain that her daughter didn't get the starring role in the ballet recital, but I needed to be polite because I was striving for a normal life filled with play dates for Danielle. The deal was, it wasn't Jane's fault that she was a perfectionist and wanted her daughter to be perfect. If I didn't live in the world of autism, I probably would have had the same expectations for all three of our kiddos. The problem was me. I just didn't give a shit anymore. I saw what "imperfection" was and all I wanted was for our youngest child to make progress in language and social interaction, not perfect it.

While I was busy balancing my socializing personalities with the neighborhood Moms, finances were still very tight. David and I had only 1 car, so I was trying to figure out a way to make more money to get a 2nd car. I was walking the kids in our double stroller everywhere and it was getting really hard, especially on rainy days, where I would pick up Gregory from school and have us all walking in the rain. I will say that at times of need, God had sent me two earth angel Moms who saw me walking in the rain with all 3 kids one day and from that day on, they would call me on rainy days and tell me they would pick up Gregory from school and bring him home so we didn't have to walk in the rain- *thank you for your love and support: Monica and Katherine!* It was kindness and actions from these Moms that would give me a boost of hope and energy to keep moving forward.

I looked into daycare for the younger kids and found that was a whole new road of rejection. Once I would tell the Mother's day out (tried 2 of those) or the daycare (tried 4 of those) that Jonathan doesn't talk much and he might have the challenges of autism, they didn't let us enroll. The daycares were privately owned and since autism wasn't a "disease" but a behavior, the daycares found technicalities to deny Jonathan, and that made it very hard to try and get a job outside the home.

This was a very telling lesson on how the world perceived our son in 2002, because people were already rejecting Jonathan. We had our fair share of events happen at local stores. We were asked to leave a kid's hair cut store because Jonathan wouldn't keep his head still during his hair cut, then he started screaming from his chair and the hair stylist threw her hands in the air and demanded, "You are going to have to leave." We did.

We were asked to leave a restaurant when Jonathan was throwing a "scream-fest" during our meal and it was upsetting other patrons. We did. See, we understood the uncomfortable, loud, screams and behaviors were terrible for people to watch and observe, because it was terrible for us too. The way people would stare at our whole family with such revulsion and judgment, kept us inside and isolated for years.

I also learned not to tell people Jonathan had autism. If I could protect him from judgment for as long as possible I would do it. Because at the age of 2, he was still known as Jonathan and I felt that based off how people were already judging and rejecting him, he had his whole life to be known as the Bordelon Kid with autism. I wanted to prolong the public discovery and just let him be a little boy without a label, for as long as I could.

We were months into our "Life Flip" of autism, when a miracle came to us. I find it amazing how God works. It wasn't until years later that I realized the gift of guidance I was getting from above and the support from angels along the way. At the time, I just saw it as an opportunity that appeared to help make money at home and use my e-commerce, sales and marketing skills.

My girlfriend knew someone looking for help with his online vitamin store. He was an elderly businessman named Keith, and he did not understand e-commerce or even the Internet. I was introduced to him and he hired me to help him launch his vitamin business online. He agreed to allow me to work from home and I would go on sales calls with him if I could get the kid coverage.

While at the onset, I had no interest in vitamins and nutrition; I had to learn about the supplements because I was creating and marketing the labels for Keith's products. I had to learn what enzymes were, amino acids, and benefits of vitamin D, C, B's. Why CoQ10 was good for the cardiovascular system. I had NO IDEA, but I was starting to create the "Nutritionist Hat" to hang on My Autism Hat Rack, and eventually I would use this knowledge to help heal our baby boy.

I found some solace in work. I would break up my days and nights and succeeded in getting Keith's supplement company online. Between kid's meals, baths and playtime, I still managed to clock in 5-8 hours a day. As I was promoting supplements, I was educating myself and connecting nutritional things to my world of autism. I was learning about what vitamins helped with cognitive processing and what vitamin deficiencies attributed to misfired neurotransmitters. I learned about enzymes and how important they are to help break down proteins and fats from foods in our digestive systems. I do look back at this time as a miracle sent my way because I could have helped Keith with any business product, but that it was supplements and I would learn how nutrition was a crucial part of Jonathan's healing pathway, was a "Mimi-ism".

I worked for Keith for about 8 months, got his business up and running and made enough money to buy a used car. David's business started to take off and we were finally getting some savings back in the bank. It was time for me to say thank you and goodbye to Keith and go back to kicking autism's butt. Jonathan was doing better with behaviors and we had changed his diet, but his speech was still lacking and his cognitive processing was not progressing.

My "Hats" on autism started to accumulate and I would find new branches of my HatRack to hang them on. I was having to delve into the worlds of biology, chemistry, quantum physics, nutrition and diet, homeopathic therapies, neurological-processing mechanics, occupational therapy, speech therapy, equestrian therapy, sensory integration therapy, Applied Behavior Analysis (ABA), Bio genetics and DNA codes, biomedical lab test results to administer protocols…and that was all when he was a toddler.

I found I was consumed with getting our son out of the grips of autism and it wasn't long before I figured out that instead of pulling Jonathan out of autism, autism was pulling us in. This is a step in the "Life Flip" that every family goes through trying to bring their child out of the fog of autism. The vast unknown of "what the hell is going on" to "I'm tired, I'm drained, I don't know the answers and I just want my kid to sleep".

I was meticulous with what food Jonathan was eating and was outraged if a therapist slipped him a cookie or piece of candy just because they thought it wouldn't hurt him. I felt like I couldn't trust another caretaker to follow his diet and routine, so we rarely had any babysitters.

We learned that certain words would irritate Jonathan, so we would avoid them. I also started to figure out that Jonathan would react to the tone or vibrations of words. It was like he was a human barometer that could feel the energy of anyone he was around. If there was a TV show on that had actors yelling or arguing, Jonathan would pick up on the tone of the actors and he would start to cry or wail as if he was in trouble or sad. I believe that was why he immersed himself into videos and kid TV shows, because it was full of music, happy songs and happy characters. Also because he could control the shows with the remote; thus control the atmosphere of emotions assaulting him.

We would learn to say things in a positive manner instead of negative. So, instead of saying "no", we would say, "Let's do this instead". We were reinforcing our children to look at the glass as half full, not half empty. The kids got in the habit of looking at things with a positive spin and when I look back on raising the kids, this was a foundation that Jonathan had demanded and Gregory and Danielle were learning empathy.

I had no idea at the time, but life had become a game of strategies filled with words, emotions and avoidances. I was starting to accumulate these ingredients into a large mixing bowl that would formulate my daily dose and serving of my "Life Mix" I needed to survive.

CHAPTER 5

## ...AND THEN THE THERAPIES

*"What we achieve inwardly will change outer reality."*
-PLUTARCH

David and I were saving any money we could to start paying for therapies and evaluations. We had insurance through his job, but insurance companies did not recognize autism as a treatable disease, so going to the Doctor because your child has "autism" was not covered. I had to think "out of the box" to get any medical help. I started targeting Jonathan's physical symptoms, looking past his behaviors by taking off the label of autism. I itemized his medical ailments, so we could go see specialists that might help him:

- He had allergies = Immunologist and get tests done.
- He had gut issues and constant diarrhea = go see a GI
- He wasn't talking and he had body spasms & tics = go see a Neurologist to check for seizures
- He couldn't communicate = he needs speech.
- He was very hyper, eye contact and his vestibular was out of whack = Sensory Integration and OT

That was where I started. I researched what doctors would take Jonathan under whichever medical treatment issue he was having. I had already mentioned we started with the Immunologist and got a sense of what his immediate allergies were. Then after getting the push off to the next doctor, we went and saw Dr. Roo, another Immunologist in the area.

Dr Roo was a kind, gentle man who was the first Doctor we actually saw in person, who knew what autism was. He didn't really know how to cure it, but he wanted to try. We took a battery of tests on Jonathan that included nutritional tests to gage deficiencies, heavy metals and toxin tests to see if he had any mercury, lead, aluminum or other junk in his body. We did a genetic test focusing on his detoxification/methylation cycle, which basically showed his body was not capable of detoxifying pollutants and free radicals.

We were introduced to the CSA (Composite Stool Analysis) test aka- the Poop Test. This is another huge milestone in parent's life raising a child with autism. You have no idea how far you will go for your child's well being until you have to secure a stool and urine sample from your child first thing in the morning. It is a wrestling match at a bare butt level of aim, non-contamination and scoop-age. The CSA test was to find out what bacteria, yeast or varmints lived inside your child's gut and colon. Yep, a glamorous life I led. After paying thousands, yes thousands, of dollars on these tests because insurance wouldn't cover "alternative testing", we finally had a semblance of our child's biomarkers and it was horrendous.

*This is where I get excited about the medical community of today (2013). I have seen it expand with more "out-of-the-box" approaches and testing to find answers of biomedical ailments for thousands of children. Alternative doctors have studies that are being researched and read by mainstream doctors and I have seen it move into a positive direction in the last 10 years, but we have more ground to cover and more answers to expose.*

We left Dr. Roo's office with test results and a supplement list of 22 supplements to give our 3 year old, 3 times a day. David and I called it the "shotgun approach" and of course we couldn't give him all of the supplements at once, nor did we want to. The dosages were even too much for me to take once a day. We started slow and saw some gains and some regressions. The important lesson I got from the 5 years we saw this doctor was I was going to be Jonathan's practitioner, researcher, nurse and data recorder. I was very grateful to Dr. Roo for accepting our child as a patient and always willing to try new approaches to treatments.

We went to a Gastro Intestinal Doctor at Children's Medical who pushed on his stomach and said he was fine. In 2003, I was a Warrior Mama in the making, and refused to leave the doctor's office until he did an X-ray on our son's GI tract. I knew he had GI issues because nothing coming out from that end of our son was normal. After Dr Russet decided to appease this vocal Mama, he came back to the exam room and apologized. He was shocked to see immense impactment of crap in the two upper corners of Jonathan's poop shoot tract. He prescribed ex lax and miralax for two weeks to move things out.

I needed to delve into the world of Speech and Occupational Therapies so we found out about a state funded organization called Early Childhood Intervention (ECI) when Jonathan was 2 ½. I had never heard of them before and when a friend of a family member casually mentioned the state service as an option, I contacted ECI immediately. None of the doctor's offices we had been to for the past 2 years had ever mentioned ECI to us. This was crucial in my endeavor to help parents down the road. We lost over a year of potential therapy help because doctors did not educate their patients on services.

The ECI therapists would come to the house, which was great, and affordable. We had a wonderful young lady by the name of Brooke who helped guide me into the world of sensory overload and help me understand how Jonathan was feeling sensory overload most of the time. ECI evaluated Jonathan and decided he needed speech too, so a girl named Julie tag teamed with Brooke and for 1 hour a week, Jonathan was getting his first therapies. Our little Jman was finally getting help from someone besides me who knew more about autism challenges in toddlers. I was starting to see progress.

I was feeling a little less alone in this journey. I was getting help from ECI and addressing medical issues that the doctors didn't have answers for, but were ruling things out like seizures or tumors. I was feeling progress in the uncharted waters of autism and I had moments of happiness glimmer through with Jonathan.

One night, or really one morning at 3:10 am, Jonathan was up. This was not a rare occurrence, as a matter of fact, Jonathan got up most nights that I could remember at 3:10 am. Of course our earlier doctors said that is was nothing out of the ordinary, but my other two kids never did it after a certain age. When he was months old, I would rock him back to sleep for hours sitting up because anytime I would lay him down, he would start crying again. Years later I figured out it was because of his reflux/gastritis issues, but back then I was clueless and only knew he was not hungry and we had gone through the mycolin gas drops by the bottle full, with no relief in pain. He and I would finally be exhausted and fall asleep in the rocking chair sitting up because it was his most comfortable position. So whenever I heard him making noise in the middle of the night, I always went to check on him.

That morning, I opened the door slowly to his room and found him standing on his mattress, holding on the edge of the crib, looking up at the corner of the room and he was laughing. Laughing, his gut giggles that made him so happy. I came into the room and looked up at the ceiling for a flying bug or light or something to see what he was fixated on and laughing at so hard. But there was nothing there.

"Jonathan, what are you looking at?" I asked him and he just kept looking at the corner of the ceiling and laughing so hard that it made me smile out of sheer joy for him.

I walked over and checked his diaper and bedding; it was dry and his crib was fine. But he was a giggle box revved up in the early morning hour. I kissed his head and laid him down, covered him up and went back to bed. A few seconds later I heard the crib springs bouncing and Jonathan laughing again. I rolled over and went to sleep with the melody of his laughter, instead of his cries, and the image of my Mimi came into my mind. I didn't think much more about this occurrence until a few weeks later during a Speech session with Julie from ECI.

Julie was asking Jonathan to identify pieces and complete a wooden puzzle they were working on. Jonathan was doing his best to make sounds that resembled the bus, car, fire engine, train and airplane. Julie held up the train piece and asked Jonathan, "Jonathan, what is this?" after silence from Jonathan, she continued, "Is this a truck?"

"Iieeee" Jonathan responded with a laugh. Julie's eyebrow shot up and she looked at me. I was shocked that he didn't say the word "no". It was one of the few words he did say and used appropriately. Before she could say anything, I responded in total explanation mode, "Julie, I know he knows the word. He is just being silly. He has been saying 'iieee' for a couple of weeks now and then giggling about it. I have no idea what it means."

Julie smiled and asked me, "Who speaks Japanese in the house?"

"Japanese? No one. We are trying to master English with him" I said in a joking, but honest answer.

"He is telling me "no" in Japanese," she said with a smile. "Watch".

Julie picked up the car puzzle piece and asked "Jonathan, is this a choo choo?"

Jonathan was reaching for the car puzzle piece and said "iieeee" with a giggle and then said, "Vroom vroom".

I was floored. He was saying "iieee" as his answer, but Julie knew it was a word, much less a Japanese word, used correctly.

"No one speaks Japanese and he doesn't watch any Japanese TV shows or videos. The only person who spoke any Japanese was my Grandmother Mimi."

"Well then maybe she taught Jonathan the word "no" in Japanese?" Julie asked hopeful to have solved the source.

"Not unless she has been teaching him from heaven." I answered with a smile and then it hit me. The night in his crib when he was laughing and looking up at the ceiling. I am always feeling my Mimi around me, but was that it? Was Jonathan seeing Mimi, his great grandmother? Was he hearing her?

Julie looked at me and smiled and said, "I wouldn't put anything past Jonathan and what he can and can't do." That was the first encouragement about Jonathan I had heard from any doctor or therapist in our autism journey.

"I couldn't agree more." I said and in my heart I had my comfortable, familiar feeling of Mimi wash over me and I thought, wow. You wonderful lady trying to connect with my baby in his fog-filled world. I felt comfort in knowing this possible occurrence, to be true. That night, I said a prayer to Mimi to keep watching over Jonathan, but to please teach him English and let's go from there.

Jonathan stopped saying the word "iiieee" as a response to questions and soon we were labeling items around the house, objects of interest and saying, "Yes, ok, or you're right." I felt my spiritual growth getting stronger along side my son's progress and more and more Mimi-isms occurred through the years.

One of the medical doctors we needed to see for Jonathan was a Neurologist and do a MRI and an over night sleep study at the hospital to rule out seizures. This experience was horrendous and the

Neurologist was a jerk. Dr. Upchuck kept us waiting for an hour for our first visit, which if you have a neurotypical child is a long time, but when you have a hyper, frustrated and hungry ASD child, it was exhausting. Then when we got into the exam room he looked at me and said, "Your son has autism."

My reply was, "Yes, I know, " but my thoughts were, "No shit Sherlock".

Then without missing a beat he said, "What do you want me to do about it?"

I was stunned about his entire approach. A Neurologist was suppose to understand or at least try to figure out why our son's brain wasn't functioning normal. Of course, by this time, I was trying to be better at keeping my "inside voice" tame, but my Warrior Mama came out and I replied, "I don't know, you're the Doctor, but you don't have to be such an ass about it."

I was exasperated from trying to keep Jonathan on my lap and I couldn't believe I had been waiting over an hour, much less paying to listen to this jerk. He looked at me and said, "Fine. We will set up a MRI and sleep study, but we won't find anything. His results will come back normal and he will still have autism."

I can tell you, even to this date, that if I were ever going to punch out a medical professional on this journey, it would have been this guy. I got up to leave and he started writing stuff on his notepad and without another word, we went to the check out counter and that was my introduction to Neurology and autism.

We scheduled the MRI for a Friday morning and the sleep study for the following Monday evening at the hospital and didn't have to see Dr. Upchuck there, thank goodness.

The MRI was scary. David, Jonathan, my Dad and I walked into a sterile, clinical hospital room and I could feel Jonathan's fears and he could feel mine. He dutifully jumped up on the sheeted gurney and was getting anxious when the IV pole was being rolled over to the bed. I held his hand to reassure him everything was going to be all right, but knowing inside everything felt like a crap-shoot and I had no idea what to expect.

The nurse came over to stick the IV needle into Jonathan's arm and he freaked out a little. He had done so many bio tests in his young life, he knew the prick pain coming. I started to rub his head with my other hand and sang, "Twinkle Twinkle Little Star" to him to calm his nerves and mine. It was the first time Jonathan was going to be put under general anesthesia and I was not ready to see my son looking at me one minute with complete fear in his eyes and then going totally lax and unconscious the next.

I was overcome by sobs seeing his motionless little body, as they took Jonathan into the MRI room where they were going to take pictures of his brain. The Anesthesiologist, Doctor Davison, was amazing. He was kind and assured me that Jonathan was still alive and breathing. He said we could stay in the area and wait, so David, my Dad and I stood there in the 15-20 minutes it took to take the MRI.

I was not prepared to see Jonathan getting "knocked out". I mean I knew about the procedure, but you are never ready to see your child be alert one minute and then comatose the next. I remember wiping the snot and tears from my face and I turned to David and whispered,

"I've never seen his body so still and at rest before." David hugged me tight and just nodded in agreement. He was being very strong for me because I was falling apart.

Dr. Davison opened the door to the MRI room and wheeled the bed with a sleeping Jonathan out to us. He said everything went great and he should be coming out of his sleep in about an hour. The next step was to wheel him up to a hospital room for recovery.

It was at that time that I had the thought to ask Dr. Davison for pictures of Jonathan's MRI. He said that our Neurologist, Dr. Upchuck, would be giving those to us and I looked at Dr. Davison and said, "I don't like Dr. Upchuck and I want to see my son's brain."

Dr. Davison smiled and turned and went back into the MRI room. A few minutes later he came out with a 10 x12 large manila envelope with the letters M.R.I. on it. "Here are copies but you need to go over it with your doctor."

I was so grateful to Dr. Davison and the lesson for me there was to ASK. If I hadn't asked, I never would have seen my son's MRI results because in the days and weeks that followed, Dr. Upchuck never returned my calls to go over Jonathan's tests from our $3,000 MRI scan. He never sent us a report. The only information I got from his office was from a nurse on the phone who told me Jonathan's MRI came back normal.

The over night sleep study was horrible on Jonathan. We had to keep him hooked up to electrodes attached all over his head, arms, torso and legs with adhesive for a 12-hour session. David stayed home with the big kids and my Dad actually came to the hospital to sit with me. I was so appreciative for him to be there and it was on this visit that my Dad actually saw what I dealt with as a parent to a child suffering with autism challenges in a 12-hour window.

It was hard to see my Dad observe me taking care of our terrified little boy. Jonathan couldn't control his anxieties or find his words to express his fears and frustrations. He was a hopper and a runner, and being contained to a bed with electrodes for hours was not Jonathan's idea of fun. One of the things that happened that night was my awareness of my Dad's patience and love he has for Jonathan. Dad was seeing Jonathan in one of his worst states of fear, exhaustion, anger and vulnerability and all I could think was what a failure I was as a parent.

I looked at my Dad and I was so angry at the unjust of it all. Why did our little Jonathan have to suffer so? My Dad hugged me and I broke down that night, yet again. I felt like I had failed Jonathan, my husband, my children, myself. I don't know how I had failed, but I did.

I had this overwhelming sense of guilt for the circumstances in our life. I could look back at the day in the Amarillo clinic when Jonathan was 3 months old and the nurse gave him 3 shots, but the shots were bundled into a DTaP, IPV, Hib, Heb B concoction totaling 7 vaccinations in one 3 month old baby's body. And he had gotten so sick with whooping cough and rashes. Why did I not know better? I trusted with blind faith the pediatrician's vaccine schedule, yes, but I had the guilt of following their demands. It was killing me inside.

I had gotten Jonathan calmed down for a twilight of sleep by 1:30 a.m. and I crawled into the hospital bed with him careful not to knock any of the electrodes off his body. My Dad laid his 6'4" frame into the recliner chair and for a few peaceful hours I heard the soft snoring of my son and my Dad alongside the beeping of the monitors recording my son's brain activity to track seizures in his sleep.

At 6:30 am, a nurse came into the room to let us know we could be discharged before their shift change at 7:00. I asked what the results looked like and the nurse couldn't tell me, but said he saw nothing "unusual". Again, so glad I asked the nurse, because we never got a report from Dr. Upchuck's office about the sleep study either.

We left the hospital and I hugged my Dad tight and he told me I was a wonderful Mother. That was something I needed to hear.

It is terrible how the Neurology experiences were so intense yet yielded no information to help us understand the effects autism had on Jonathan's brain.

In later years, I found a great Neurologist who was the complete opposite of Upchuck. We were part of an Abilify Study for children on the autism spectrum monitored by Dr. Sperry, who was kind, informative, and talked to Jonathan, not about him, in his presence. Dr. Sperry put some faith back into my views of the mainstream medical community. This was the only SSRI protocol we did with Jonathan and we did see good results in calming effects for about 6 months. After 6 months, a weight gain of 13 pounds and some new facial tics surfacing, we didn't see any more benefits to the drug, so we started to wean him off and continued to treat Jonathan with natural supplements and Young Living Essential Oils[2].

My "Hat" collection was getting larger and my knowledge of medical specialties and therapies was expanding onto new branches of my HatRack.

---

[2] See Part II – Chapter 19: My "Essential Oils & Autism Hat"

CHAPTER 6

## FINDING MY "HOPE HAT"

*"Optimism is the faith that leads to achievement.
Nothing can be done without hope and confidence."*
-HELEN KELLER

Hope is what eventually got my ass off the shower floor of my bathroom, as the water was rushing down on my head, mixing with the uncontrollable sobs and tears that racked my body. This particular day was my birthday and it had taken a few years, but the ugly, boo-hoo cry was happening.

Jonathan was almost 3 years old and had just had an extreme "scream-fest" that had lasted over 30 minutes. He had screamed until he was hoarse and his eyes were swollen from his tears. He had successfully extracted a few handfuls of my hair, given me 2 new bite marks, bruises on my arms and face and had my ears "ringing" from his screams. I had expected the police to be knocking at the door any minute because I just knew his screams could be heard miles away.

After Jonathan had calmed down, the only thing I had the energy to do was get in the shower and try and wash the agony of autism away. This was a hard time for Jonathan. His frustrations were so extreme because he couldn't communicate well with anyone. I tried hard to "decode" his wants and needs before he would "lose it", but sometimes I was not fast enough and he would just start crying.

This was also my most overwhelming time with Jonathan and autism. He would have those beautiful, hazel eyes briefly stare into mine trying so hard to communicate his feelings. Can you imagine?

Having all your thoughts locked up inside of you and knowing people can not understand what you are trying to tell them? It was heartbreaking. We were so excited his eye contact was getting stronger, but then having to see the pain and loneliness reflected in his eyes was agonizing.

To help with communication, we would have pictures of items labeled all over the house so he could easily pick up a picture and show me what he wanted: an apple, or video or the park to go swing. But that morning, there were no picture cards to identify his pain and frustration of trying to communicate his dilemma.

I knew Jonathan was smart and not mentally void, as the doctors had claimed him to be. I knew he was trying so hard to tell me how he felt and what he was thinking. He amazed me at 2 ½, when he started to take his letter blocks and blue magnet alphabet letters and spell out videos he loved to watch. His first spelled word with his blocked letters was *Nick Jr.* laid out on the floor. I had asked Danielle if she had done that and she said "No".

Then I called Jonathan over and asked him, "Jonathan, did you spell this?" and he looked up at me with a huge smile and said "Nick Jr!". WHAT?!?! Jonathan, our limited-verbal, autistic child had taught himself how to spell and read! He had memorized the alphabet from TV shows and a VTech letter table he played on all the time. I just thought he was hitting buttons, but this amazing boy was teaching himself the alphabet and how to spell words he liked!

That is why things were could be so hard. Even with our progress, Jonathan could have a "scream-fest" over things we couldn't identify and fix fast, or something I would have to search for, figure out or "decode". This particular day, I obviously hadn't "decoded" fast enough for Jonathan to tell me how he felt or what was wrong. It was like a vicious cycle of "great days" and "bad days".

As the water was rushing down onto my head in my shower escape pod, I was going over the events in my head and I just could not figure out why he had gotten so upset. He and I were drawing pictures and he loved to do that. We had Veggie Tales on the TV and everything was great, then Jonathan looked me in the eyes and just started to scream in extreme pain. He ran to the couch and threw himself over the arm and just kept crying. I went to console him and the Tasmanian devil replaced my son. He went wild at the slightest touch and my voice irritated him. His face was so red, I was afraid he would "pop".

I quickly implemented some sensory techniques the ECI therapist had taught me:

> **1.** Brush his forearms with a soft bristle brush - I grab the bristle therapy brush and started to stroke the brush down from his shoulder to his wrist...then he grabbed the brush from me and bit the sucker in half.
>
> **2.** Try and give him a tight hug for pressure - This seemed to help him, but after 2 deep bite marks into my shoulder I had to release him and he went from the couch to flaying on the floor.
>
> **3.** I got down to his eye level and started saying "safe words" that resonated with him and would help distract his thoughts of pain: happy", "grapes", "Larry-Boy", "Silly Songs"...this tactic worked as it seemed to distract his mind to cheerful thoughts and from the physical pain he was feeling.

When he started to calm down, I cradled him in my lap and rocked him for what seemed an eternity. Exhausted, he passed out. I was looking down at his peaceful, angelic face as he was sleeping in my arms and I placed him on the floor with pillows surrounding his body and went to my shower escape pod. What triggered the pain? A tummy ache, the TV, the color pencil he was using, my singing...what? And what made it so hard was that he couldn't tell me. I couldn't help him and my "Decoder Hat" was off frequency - I was **HOPELESS**...

> *HOPELESS*...that is what I felt as the water came down over my head in the shower.
> *HOPELESS*...for answers from non-existent doctors.
> *HOPELESS*...for the lack of finances, as we could never afford all the therapies, supplements, or protocols he needed to heal.
> *HOPELESS*...to ever find a Preschool that would accept us.
> *HOPELESS*...for our other 2 children having to deal with this roller coaster ride of autism.
> *HOPELESS*...that Jonathan would ever be pain-free.
> *HOPELESS*...to ever hear Jonathan say the words:
> "I love you Mama".

That was the kicker and my tears started flowing and my butt found the hard, tile floor and I didn't care anymore.

The only thing that pulled me from my sob-fest was the water started getting cold. My butt hurt, I was soaked, my heart was broken and I was empty again – Happy Birthday to me.

As I stood up, I thought: "Well, shit! This just sucks." I was pissed-off (again). I wanted to have a "scream-fest". I wanted to curse the "cause" because this autism crap was horrific. It was hurting my baby, my family...me! You know what, I am tired of autism kicking my ass; it was my turn to kick autism's ass. I turned the water off, grabbed a towel, and looked in the mirror and the answer to my questions was staring right back at me. I was the answer. It was up to me to heal Jonathan because this family was all Jonathan had.

I could not fall apart now. He needed me and I needed strength. I was getting drained from society's negative "outcomes" for Jonathan. I needed to turn it around - I needed **HOPE**!

*HOPE* is a frame of mind.
*HOPE* is positive.
*HOPE* is customized.
*HOPE* is free.
*HOPE* is boundless.
*HOPE* is a simple word with a POWERFUL sense of courage.

I finished my pity party in the bathroom and put on my big girl panties. Enough. I was tired of not having more information and help with this mess. I was tired of trying to cure autism on my own. I was going to find parents who had kids with autism and start a support group. I knew I could not be the only parent in my area with this situation. I was going to go find parents I could relate to and learn from.

That very day I received a Mimi-ism that came by way of my Mother. She had sent me a birthday package in the mail and when I opened it, my heart smiled. My Mom had sent me a beautiful necklace with a gold and silver charm in the shape of an awareness ribbon. Across the ribbon was the word: **HOPE**

I called my Mom and told her how grateful I was for her gift and her timing was brilliant.

OK, Autism world… Now I was ready…my "Hope Hat" was on!

CHAPTER 7

## GRAB A BOWL AND MAKE YOUR "LIFE MIX"

*"It only takes one spoiled ingredient to ruin an entire recipe."*
               -MAUREEN BRICE BORDELON

I was ready to kick autism's ass and have it stop kicking mine. I needed to make sure I had all the ammo and the right ingredients to pour into my body, mind and soul. I thought of it as a mush pot of assorted strengths and knowledge poured into a big bowl to make a thriving "life mix".

When I changed the ingredients of my life mix, something amazing started to happen. I noticed that I was starting to heal along side of Jonathan. Happiness was a common emotion and joy was filling our house again. I knew that there was nothing to gain from being negative and everything started to move forward.

The first 3 years of Jonathan's life had taught me so much. David and I were officially parents of an "extra needs" child and we were dealt a challenging hand in this life. So having three kids and raising them to be independent, loving, happy individuals was my job. And I knew I was doing a pretty good job because my toughest critics said I was great- Gregory and Danielle.

But what about Jonathan? What did he feel and how do we raise a child with tremendous challenges to live a happy, independent, fulfilling life? I knew that the values and foundation of how we choose to raise our children and the ingredients in my life mix would also help make our children's life mix. Gregory, Danielle and Jonathan would feed off of our energy, examples and knowledge.

I was changing my stance from a Mother of a Damaged Victim to Hopeful Healer. I started to create and wear my "PMS Hat" (Positive Mind Set)[3].

I wanted recovery for Jonathan but what was recovery? When he was younger there were no kids recovering from autism and most therapies were all behavior, not biomedical. So I decided to define a path of healing with goals of making Jonathan's pain go away, communication build and happiness maintained.

I had already figured out that my "controlling issues" were not very helpful and most times set us all up for failed outcomes. What I could control was Jonathan's environment and help set it up for daily successes. I would label items throughout the house, give him his supplements that would help with his digestion and allergies, and make sure he had the right food to eat.

What I couldn't control, were circumstances outside of his "bubble". I couldn't control how people would react to his tics, squeals and hopping. I couldn't control the weather and if the barometric pressure was hurting his head causing a migraine. I couldn't control if the therapists or teacher had a bad day and were going to bring the "negative" vibe into the house or classroom. The only thing I could control was my life mix.

I had to make sure I kept my life mix bowl filled with the right ingredients so I filled my mind and soul up with:

*Love, Hope, Understanding, Empathy, Patience, Joy and a Positive Mind Set (PMS).*

---

[3] See PART II – Chapter 16: My "PMS Hat"

**Instead of thinking the "worst case scenario" I would visualize a successful outcome supported by *love*, guided by *hope* and manifesting a *joyous* outcome.**

This was huge for me because I would always prepare an outing with Jonathan with an escape plan in mind in case of the unforeseen failure of the adventure. For example: When we would go to an indoor, inflatable jump house place, I would pack 3 sets of snacks for him so he wouldn't try and swipe another kid's Teddy grahams. I would survey the layout of the establishment for all possible exit doors because our little dude would find the one I hadn't seen and set off the fire door alarm (yes, this happened once or twice). I would stick to him like glue to make sure he didn't shove or cut in line going through the net entranceways or up the slides, because we were still learning to take turns.

What I thought I was doing was being prepared for the "things that will go wrong". What I found out I really was doing was putting negative energy into gear and visualizing things "to go wrong" and so 85% of the time they did. The good thing was, I was prepared for it. The bad thing was, that I went into the adventure with a negative mind set supporting Jonathan's failure and he felt it. More times than not, the exit strategies ended in a "scream-fest/melt-down" and I would have to throw him over my shoulder and try to make it to the car with most of my hair intact.

When I started to change my mind set to a successful adventure outcome I would still pack 3 sets of snacks but it was because I knew he might eat all of them. I would stand in one place and not follow him around so he could explore and gain independence, still knowing I was there at the jump house if he needed me. I would start giving him time references that gave him control of the options of leaving in 10 minutes or 15 minutes.

Jonathan had shown me no signs of him understanding time, but after a few tries, he understood he had control of when we would leave in the reference range of 10 or 15 minutes. Soon he was putting on his shoes and walking out the door with me instead of over my shoulder. I loved these small steps to compliance.

**Instead of "Jonathan can't do that" I was thinking of all the things "Jonathan can do" and focusing on his strengths to build his self-esteem using *patience* and my *PMS Hat*.**

This was the game changer in helping Jonathan with his behaviors and my reactions to his behaviors. For way too long I looked at Jonathan as if his glass was half empty drained by autism. How freaking unfair that was. Here was a beautiful, little soul who each day of his life was trying so hard to communicate, feel good, love everyone and survive.

I never would tear him down, but I realized that I was correcting his "no-no's" or "hiccups" all the time rather than building up his accomplishments. I thought I was helping him learn the right way to do things. This had worked with our other two kids, why not Jonathan? Well, simple - because he wasn't like our other two kids and he knew it. He was wired differently and he had sensitive neurological and nervous systems that were on overload or hyperdrive.

Jonathan didn't see me as teaching him, he saw me as another obstacle to his growth. I know he felt my love, but he wanted my approval and support on his adventures, not my guidance.

I learned in Applied Behavior Analysis (ABA) and $40,000 later, not to encourage bad behavior by ignoring it. However, since I was applying the ABA therapy approach, Jonathan's interpretation was that 90% of everything he was doing was bad because he didn't follow rules or wouldn't comply most times. In our experience, traditional ABA actually escalated Jonathan's bad behaviors instead of decreased them, but in a year's timeframe, he understood compliance.

*(ABA is known to work for many children on the Autism Spectrum, so always remember to go with your gut on what therapy approaches work best for your family. Adding RDI techniques with our ABA program provided our best results.)*

We were on our 3rd round of potty training, which is hell for any child with autism and their parents, and I had been following my ABA methods without much success. Jonathan was 3 ½ years old, and after 6 long months, we had finally gotten the pee tactics down- yea!!! But the poop strategies were not happening.

I went to a local workshop by a woman named Brenda M. Batts, who had written a book called, Road to Independence[4]. Brenda had a Special Education background, specializing in behavior management, but most important to me, she had a son with autism. She could relate to the journey I was on. Her workshop was wonderful and in her book, she had devoted a chapter to potty training. *(In later years, Brenda wrote the book* Ready, Set, Potty! *focusing on potty training "extra needs" children.)*

Brenda's method was to use visual pictures of the potty, sink, clothes, and an itemized schedule/report of bathroom events. But what I loved is she stressed to make the bathroom environment a party of celebration and achievement. She encouraged praise for all actions on the potty adventure. Finally, over a Thanksgiving weekend, Jonathan had a successful "movement" on the potty and boy did we celebrate! There were "hiccups" in the weeks to follow of "poop art" on the

---

[4]See References: Brenda M. Batts

bathroom walls and tub, but I looked at it as a step forward; he was using his eye-hand coordination. Within a month, Jonathan was a completely independent potty-trained success story- Booyah!

I liked the structure of ABA, but not the harsh consequences. I knew there had to be a better way to help our son with compliance without having him escalate into a scream-fest for 20 minutes before he complied and then got a reward.

I explored Relationship Development Intervention (RDI). There were no centers in our area at the time, so I delved into studying and implemented RDI techniques into our in-home ABA program. This is where I really had to wear a lot of hats. Every child afflicted with the symptoms of autism has a varying degree of impairments and I believe there needs to be a customized approach for each child. ABA might really help one child, while RDI helps another. I took the strengths of many therapies and customized Jonathan's therapy structure.

I would praise, not discourage his hand flapping telling him to "fly higher" and "be excited". Then, I would be the crazy looking Mom hand flapping with her kid at the playground. Pretty soon even Jonathan got tired of my hand flapping with him, so it decreased.

I would watch him draw imperfect circles and squares when we would work on shapes and colors and tell him "Great job on your curves and lines!"

Jonathan would run, hop and jump in lieu of walking, so instead of correcting him, I would skip right by his side. He started to look at me like I was nuts, but I did it with a smile and a laugh and he loved it.

What I noticed was he started to connect to me, instead of running from me. He would mirror my actions of slowing down or walking and eventually he held my hand. It wasn't until he reached for my hand on his own, did I realize he had never done it. Now that was a moment of love and trust from Jonathan.

**I really despised people judging my child, or me, so I had to change my frame of mind to: "Thank God my child has our love & understanding" and I did this with the help of our older two kids,** *patience, empathy* **and** *love.* **We even named one event:**

### *"The Moses Moment"*

The 2004 school year was starting and I needed to go to Target for school supplies. David was out of town on business and the kids were too young to be left at home alone. Now remember, David and I were still doing the "taking turns to the store" tactics, so I knew I was playing with fire attempting this trip, but school supplies were in need.

I piled the kids into the car and headed to Target with my PMS Hat firmly on my head. We made it to the school supply section towards the back of the store and Jonathan was buckled in the shopping cart while the two older kids were grabbing pencils, pens, protractors and construction paper.

The area was jam-packed with other neighborhood Moms I recognized and we were all scrambling to fill our baskets with items from the mandatory lists. There was a school supply display in the middle of the area that was about 8 feet high with piles of loose-leaf paper and boxes of folders. Hanging from the ceiling was a giant cut out of a cartoon man in the shape of scissors and had the Target logo on it.

I had taken my eyes off of Jonathan to look at some crayons Danielle was showing me she wanted, when I heard a little girl yell, "Wow, look at that boy climb so high!"

My heart stopped, and the hairs on the back of my neck stood up. I knew it was our Jonathan the little girl was talking about. I turned and sure enough, Jonathan had unbuckled his cart-belt from the cart like Houdini, and escaped up to the piles of paper and started pulling at the cartoon, scissor- man display.

Every step he took, he would send paper flying in all directions. I told Danielle to stay put and I started to climb up the stacks of paper to get Jonathan down. A Target clerk appeared out of nowhere and started to tell me, "Excuse me, but he can't do that. You need to get him down." Then the clerk looked up at Jonathan, " Hey little guy, stop hanging on that display."

I didn't respond to the clerk because I was trying to figure out a "PMS phrase" to get Jonathan down as I reached up and grabbed his foot. His shoe came off, and he squirmed to the other side of the display onto more mountains of paper. I climbed back down and ran to the other side of the display to reach him, when I saw the Target clerk try and grab Jonathan by the leg. I know the clerk was just trying to do his job, but I also knew that if he grabbed Jonathan, Jonathan would freak out and be terrified by a stranger grabbing him.

Too late. The sound was like the emergency sirens you hear when there is a tornado coming. Slow and low but rising to an ear, splitting tone that makes you cover your ears to save your senses. The sound was coming from my son as he tried to free his leg from the grasp of the Target clerk pulling him down from the hanging display and piles of paper. At this point, I had no PMS phrases in my head. All I could think of was I wanted Wonder Woman's invisible plane to appear and fly myself and my children out of Target ASAP!

I reached the other side of the mountain of papers and picked up Jonathan, freeing him from the Target clerk's grasp. I held him tight to my chest as he was biting down on my shoulder and slapping me in my face and ears while still managing to scream in such a shrill that my ears didn't stop ringing for hours later.

Gregory had heard the siren screams and by this stage in our lives, he knew the drill. I looked at him and said, "Get the cart, get my purse, get your sister- let's go".

I was looking around for Danielle and found her still frozen in her spot by the crayons. I saw Gregory reach his hand out to Danielle and guide her to the cart close to the aisle. The mothers I had been nodding to and saying hello just moments before, were looking at me in utter horror and physically shielding their children from my family. They were muttering things like, "Oh my god, can't she control him", "What a devil child", "Spoiled little brat".

All I wanted to say back to these miserable bitches was, "Fuck you", but my parents would be proud to know, I didn't.

The entire event went in slow motion in my mind. As I was taking it all in, I was mortified. I was ashamed of my youngest child, horrified for my older two kids to hear the nasty things these mothers were saying out loud and as I maneuvered my way to the main aisle with Jonathan screaming and slapping me, I was ready to burst into tears, but I wouldn't give the on lookers the satisfaction of seeing me defeated.

I asked God to give me the strength to make it to the front doors without crying. I sucked in my breath, tuned out the screams deafening my eardrums, and held tight to my surprisingly strong, thrashing 3 year old and started walking.

I maneuvered one foot in front of the other, alongside Gregory who had my purse on his shoulder, his sister's hand helping him steer the cart full of school supplies and the four of us began making our way down the main aisle of Target. Jonathan's screams were gathering people towards the main aisle of the store and what happened next was amazing.

As I glanced past arms flying across my face, I saw Gregory and Danielle, and I had a calm come over me of pure strength. Jonathan felt the vibe with each step I took and he stopped kicking and slapping and his siren screams quieted to a loud howl. I didn't rush my family down the red-painted aisle of Target, but instead walked slow and looked down at Gregory and Danielle and smiled at them. I was so proud of how they were handling themselves and so grateful to them for what they had to put up with in their daily lives.

We walked slow and purposely down the aisle and more and more people gathered to stare at us. I kept smiling because the image of what was unfolding was making me laugh. I leaned over to Gregory and Danielle and said, "Hey, look kids, Jonathan is like Moses and has parted the Target Red Sea." Every step we took down the red colored aisle, people who had come out to see what all the screaming was about and stare at us, would move back out of our way as if we were parting the Red Sea to get to the promise land of the front doors…and it worked. I glanced at Gregory and Danielle and they were smiling at my joke and I knew for a brief moment, I had evaporated the humiliation of events unfolding, for my two older kiddos.

I told Gregory to leave the cart full of school supplies by the check out counter and we walked through the electronic doors leaving the onlookers, bitchy mothers and the Target Red Sea behind us.

I was straining to keep my smile on for the kids and make it to the car when I felt a hand on my arm. It was my neighbor Pamela. She was saying something but I couldn't hear her because my ears were ringing and Jonathan was still howling. I shook my head at her and said, "Pamela, I can't hear you, I have to go."

She leaned closer to me and said, "Can I help you? Do you need me to get you anything from inside Target?"

Well, God had answered my prayer to give me strength not to cry in front of all the Target onlookers and make it to the exit doors. That a Mimi-ism was waiting for me in the form of a kind neighbor reaching out to help me in a crisis, not judge me or my child, was all it took and I couldn't stop the tears from forming in my eyes. I gave her a thankful smile and said, "No, but thank you anyway Pamela, I have to go, but thank you for wanting to help." I read Pamela's lips respond "Ok" and she smiled as I turned to pack the kids into the car and went home.

The kids remember that day as the "Moses Moment" in Target, but I remember that day as a valuable lesson about other people's energies. I cannot control how people will judge my family or me. I can't let their negative thoughts and energies effect me or we all lose. Even writing this story now, brings back the feelings of hurt, shame and embarrassment I felt that day, but I always reflect on how the Moses Moment ended. With a prayer to God to give me strength to get through the parting of the Target "Red Sea", and a friend reaching out with a helping hand, not judgment.

I had to let go of how I felt when others judged us in public. I was changing my parenting tactics to support Jonathan, not correct him to make me and others feel more comfortable. This was very hard to do in a conformist society, but Jonathan needed to know how much we loved him and we wanted to understand how he saw the world.

When we would go to the playground and our son was squealing and flapping his arms on the swings or slides, I had to not give a shit anymore when ignorant people would say to me, "Can't you control your son's squeals and flapping?"

I mean seriously, after a few years of getting comments like that, all I really wanted to say was "Don't you think I would if I could!" But, instead I took the positive route and would turn to the person saying it to me and calmly reply, "Be my guest. You can ask him to stop if you'd like too, but if it bothers you so much, can't you just look away."

I found this response very effective with judgmental people. Jonathan needed to flap his arms because he was happy and excited and physically needed to release his energy. He wasn't hurting anyone, but he was trying to enjoy his playtime just like any other kid, so I would let him.

I was changing the ingredients in my life mix. Instead of looking at Jonathan as a victim to autism, I looked past the challenges and hiccups and saw our beautiful child. I started to treat him as if he could do more things than he knew how. I would pour positive energy into him so he would feel good about himself and build his self-esteem. This was working and making a better life for our family. I was putting my anger and negative issues about autism aside and directing my energy to make positive things happen.

CHAPTER 8

## BREAKING IN MY "ADVOCACY HAT/HELMET"

*"Each of us must be the change we want to see in the world."*
-MAHATMA GHANDI

I looked up the word Advocate and the word "SUPPORT" was the definition. Keeping with my Positive Mind Set (PMS), I put on my "Advocacy Hat" for my family.

I was desperate to get more support from the autism community. My life-long girlfriends, the Divas, were loving and caring, but they didn't understand what I was going through. Thank God because that would mean another child with autism. I wanted to find a group of parents that understood the paths David and I were blindly navigating. I had never been to an Alcoholic Anonymous (AA) meeting, but seeing what was depicted in movies and how everyone would share their experiences, made me think I wanted to attend an AA Meeting with the AA topic being "Autism Anyone"?

I had contacted the national autism groups but only one Association had a local chapter so David and I went to a monthly get together. When we got to the meeting there were 4 Moms plus David. One mother I met there, was very knowledgeable and informative about what school services worked for her son in his treatment plan. The Mom on the left of me was new like me and she cried the whole meeting. The other mom across the table from me bitched about the school system, doctors, government and what services were not available. I learned some new things and I related to all of those women, but I had been in that negative place for too long and I didn't want to go backwards.

I did find out that the Autism Society of America's annual Autism Convention was being held in Seattle and I made up my mind to go. I called my younger sister who lived in Seattle and asked if I could crash at her house for a few days. She said yes and I booked a flight and bought my conference pass to my first autism convention in July 2004!

I arrived in Seattle and was so excited about the conference, I was an hour early. I checked in and got my badge, conference bag filled with pamphlets and product info, an exhibitors guide and a conference proceedings syllabus that was 1.5" thick. It was filled with the speakers' PowerPoint presentations and I was salivating over the book like it was a cheesy romance novel. There were Autism Specialists who were speaking about Speech Therapy, Mercury Toxicity, Sensory Integration, Special Diets, Oxidative Stress, Special Education, ABA, RDI, Floortime, Social Stories and more.

The Keynote speaker was Dr. Geraldine Dawson and I walked into the main room to find over 3,000 people already in their seats. I was shocked. Did all of these people get the "Good Luck" handshake from their pediatricians too? I looked around and the only seats available were in the middle of rows but I was too excited to be boxed in. I found one seat on the back row way in the corner and got ready to learn.

The stage was set with a huge screen next to a table and podium. The screen had the words "Soaring to New Heights" across it with the Autism Society of America's logo underneath it. Yep, I was in the right place.

There was a man who came across the stage and everyone started cheering and clapping. He reached the podium and the screen went from the ASA logo to a giant image of his face. He was a distinguished man, about 60 years old with a bright smile and tan face. He introduced himself as Rob Beck, the Chairman of ASA and then he started the conference.

It is so amusing when the Universe brings something across your path, and you are trying to figure it out. It starts with a feeling you have tugging at your conscience but you can't identify the meaning of it. While Mr. Beck was talking, I kept thinking, I know that man. I was wracking my brain trying to figure out where I had seen his face.

Was it from the ASA website? Possibly. But what I couldn't shake was that I knew his voice. Did I use to work with him in New York? No. Did I know him from my publishing days? No. I couldn't pinpoint how I knew him, but he was familiar. Rob Beck turned and introduced Dr. Dawson and I listen to her talk about genetic research pertaining to autism and her work with the University of Washington.

I looked around in awe at the thousands of people in one room, all gathered because of autism. I thought about the lack of support, funds, and insurance coverage for all of these parents and in turn, the children. But these people were here to learn like me. To make a difference in a child's life. It was overwhelming and amazing.

Dr. Dawson was finishing up her presentation and Rob Beck came back to the podium, concluded the Keynote session and then opened the doors for us all to go to speakers and exhibitors for the ASA 2004 convention. One problem, I couldn't shake the feeling that I knew Rob Beck. I snuck out the door before the thousands of people were exiting and I called my Dad back in Dallas. Luckily he answered, "Hi Marne, how is the conference going?"

"Amazing Daddy, but I have a really weird question for you. Do you know a gentleman by the name of Rob Beck?"

"Rob Beck? Sure. He and his family grew up with us in Dallas. The Becks were at our masses and holiday parties, but their children were older than you". Boom, there it was! Rob and Elizabeth Beck were family friends but the kids were older than me, so we only saw them for holiday parties every once in a while.

Then I remembered, Elizabeth and Rob Beck helped get MADD (Mother's Against Drunk Driving) on the map as the largest grassroots charity organization in the 80s and 90s. And now, here was Rob Beck as Executive Director of the Autism Society of America…now that was a Mimi-ism I had to take action on.

"Well, Daddy, Rob Beck is the Executive Director of the National ASA and just spoke at the convention. How small world is that?" I joked and my Dad agreed and I told him I would call him later.

When I walked back into the main ballroom, people were moving about and filing out of the doors to go see exhibitors and scheduled speakers in multiple conference rooms throughout the convention center. I took a deep breath and thought; "I am going to go re-introduce myself to Rob Beck." I wasn't sure if he would remember me or my family, but I needed him to know what he was doing, was helping me as a Mother and our son.

I made my way to the stage and saw Rob Beck speaking with a gentleman and there were about 3 other people waiting to talk to him. I stood in line and watched, as he was courteous and listened to another Mother thanking him for his work and the ASA for doing the convention. Mr. Beck was attentive and listened to each person, never rushing them off. He was speaking to another Mother in front of me and looked over her shoulder at me and smiled, then return to listen to the Mother talk about services and legislation in her state being terrible. They finished their conversation and I stepped forward because it was my turn.

I reached out my hand to shake Mr. Beck's and said,

"Hello Mr. Beck. I don't know if you will remember me but my name is Maureen Brice Bordelon and my parents are Bob and Susan Brice."

Rob Beck looked at me and smiled, "Maureen, of course I remember you but I haven't seen you since you were about 13," and he took my hand and pulled me in for a big bear hug. "How are your Mom and Dad?"

I returned the hug and replied, "They are wonderful. Divorced, but happy."

Then Mr. Beck looked at me and asked, "What are you doing here? Are you a Special Ed teacher or professional?" and I guess my answer was in my eyes and his faced softened and he said, "You have a child with autism?"

I nodded yes, "A beautiful little boy named Jonathan. Our third child and I flew here from Dallas for the convention to meet the speakers and learn as much as I can."

Mr. Beck took me by the shoulder and said, "Then let's make that happen, shall we."

The next three days were filled with seminars over topics I craved to learn more about: Visual Strategies for Improving Communication, Sensory Integration, Insurance Coverage, Mercury Toxicity in the brain, Neuro-cognitive Nutritional Depletions, Genetic Codes, Drug free therapy treatments for Autism, Autism Bills and Legislation and more. I saw over 20 speakers and presentations, as I learned the first day to start hopping from one to the next, gather intel and absorb.

I met exhibitors who were specialists in their fields and selling books, supplements and even bio-tests. I was strolling down one aisle and stopped when I saw Carol Gray's book about Social Stories.

Knowing I had used her book to help Jonathan with communication, I picked it up off the table and heard someone say, "That is a really great starter book for Social Stories."

I looked up and there she was, Carol Gray. I couldn't believe it. I was actually meeting the mind that helped families connect with their kids. "I love your book. I use your techniques all the time and I take real pictures and implement them into social stories to help our son communicate with his peers and teachers." My words fumbled from my lips and I finally stopped talking.

Carol Gray smiled and simply said, "I am so happy to hear that, that is why I wrote it." She and I spoke for 30 minutes about her background and how she came up with the simple social story structure. I felt like I was getting my own private seminar, and actually, I was.

I met an exhibitor from a place that did genetic testing, a company that sold Nordic fish oil, Discovery toys, sensory handmade items like blankets, backpacks and more. It was wonderful. I felt like I had stepped into an Autism Shop and I was wishing I had thousands of dollars to buy one of everything.

Rob Beck asked me to join him as his guest at the ASA opening party celebration the first night of the conference. The party was full of all the movers and shakers from the convention; speakers, exhibitors and patrons of ASA. He introduced me to Dr. Geraldine Dawson, the Keynote speaker, and I asked her how much research was being done on vaccines and the connection of cause to autism. I had no idea at the time of the huge political controversy, because I just wanted answers and information. Two things happened here. Rob Beck realized I didn't mince words and was not shy to ask questions, and Dr. Dawson was uncomfortable answering my question. She did respond that she was involved with genetic research, not vaccines. She then excused herself and I looked at Mr. Beck and said, "Well, that was uncomfortable, but I guess I got my answer."

*Years later, I read that Dr. Dawson became the Chief Science Officer at Autism Speaks (AS) in charge of research with a $24 million dollar a year budget. Dr. Dawson had access to millions of dollars raised by families dealing with autism and I have personally never read a research study from her department at AS in regards to vaccines involvement with autism.*

I went to dinner the following evening with Rob Beck and the ASA National Board members. I met Lee Grossman, President; Dr. Cathy Pratt, and a few more members of the board. One man stood out because he was a fellow Texan; Jeff Sell. Jeff was also a father of twin boys with autism and a lawyer involved with the vaccine-injured children court cases. I learned more at that dinner about the politics of autism in government and the battle to even get research done on pressing issues.

Rob Beck was trying to get a bill passed to do infant testing (much like the PKU test) at birth to see if a baby's immune system was compromised. I appreciated this test proposal as it would have been information I would have loved to have known prior to giving vaccines to all 3 of my kids. Every person at that dinner had his or her focused passion, just like me.

My third day at the conference was full of more seminars, meeting doctors, therapists, and parents. I found out, as I was thanking Mr. Beck for all of his kindness and help, that he was retiring that year from ASA. I was sad to see him retire, but so grateful for the opportunity and timeliness of it all. I went home from

Seattle with a fire in my belly. I knew our community needed support, but the immediate need was information for parents. I was giddy thinking how I had jumped on a plane to go across the country and attend an Autism Conference, not knowing a soul, but ended up meeting the Conference key players who had been making strides and efforts for the Autism Community on a national scale. The Universe was straightening out my "Life Flip" and I was ready to make things happen.

I had returned home from Seattle when I was cooking dinner, like a short order cook due to the special diets our family was eating, and the news came on. Channel 11 was highlighting a segment for an event called *Stephanie's Day* at a Dallas Mall. The word autism caught my attention and I stopped chopping veggies. *Stephanie's Day* was an event scheduled for that weekend, where local companies would be handing out information about autism and therapies available in the area. Boom! There it was again…HOPE. I was going to meet local people who lived in the autism bubble.

That Saturday morning all five of us of geared up for a day at the Mall. This was not a normal "outing" for the Bordelon Family. Remember, we did shifts on adventures because most places over whelmed Jonathan and it was hard to "blend in". Nonetheless, I wasn't going to have any of us miss *Stephanie's Day*. We got to the Dallas Mall and found the event going in full swing. There were about 20-30 tables set up with Speech Therapists, Churches with the Special Needs Programs, Special Need's Camps, Nutritionists, Occupational Therapists and more. I was walking by the second table when I saw a lady sitting by herself with a sign up sheet in front of her. I stopped and asked, "Hi, what are you peddling?" in a good-humored tone.

She looked at me and smiled and said, "Nothing, I just wanted to grab a table to have a place for parents to sign up for a local Parent Support Group."

*Ok, by now reading this book, you have to say it with me:*
**"*Mimi-ism*!"**

I took the pen from her hand and saw I would be the first parent to sign up on her sheet and I was proud to do so. "My name is Maureen and I live in Allen."

"Me too! My name is Liz and I have a son with autism who is 6 years old."

I reached behind me to David who was pushing Jonathan in the stroller and I replied, "Our son Jonathan is 4 and you and I have a lot to discuss." And we did.

A couple of weeks after *Stephanie's Day*, Liz emailed her composed parent list and arranged a support gathering at a local coffee house in Allen. 18 Moms showed up and from that 18, 5 of us Moms created a Parent Support group that included all of North Dallas. It was called the Allen-Frisco-Plano Autism Spectrum Parent Group- whew! We just called it AFP Group for short.

Kim, Beth, Arch, Liz and myself came together as Moms all with our specialties and together we organized monthly meetings for Parents to connect and relate to each other. We had Doctors come speak to our group to help educate parents about the biological effects of autism. Insurance Planners would come and help us break down insurance coverage for our therapies. We had a CPA come to help us figure out our tax breaks for out-of-pocket medical expenses and therapies.

We organized a Round-table meeting and invited therapists, doctors, the ASA chapter, School Districts Special Needs Coordinators - all to be available for parents to speak with them and ask questions.

Our AFP Group organized our first Teacher/Therapist Appreciation dinner at a restaurant Beth had some pull with and gave out awards to prominent achievers in our community.

And then we would have our "Autism Anyone" nights I had dreamed about. The ones where parents could just "dump" their crap in the mush pot without any judgment, but lots of empathy. I created a website for the AFP Group with up-to-date information to help give parents a guide to action after they got the diagnosis news. The group was developing and so was the information. Parents were comparing notes, doctors, schools, therapists and making personal connections. Autism was feeling less lonely.

The AFP Group spurred off a few more Parent support groups that focused on members with younger kids, older kids, different diet kids etc…In 2007 after 3 years of monthly meetings and supportive gatherings, AFP was being run by just Liz and I and we were ready for a break, so we took AFP completely to our online yahoo group and stopped the physical gatherings.

I have been very blessed to be a part of the parent support growth in North Texas. The strength of the Moms and Dads in our area has since progressed through the years into different parent support groups all filled with determined Warrior Parents finding answers to help heal their children.

The Advocacy Hat wasn't just worn for parent support groups. It would morph into a Helmet many times protecting me as I plowed into Special Education ARD meetings and mediations, marched in Washington to "Green our Vaccines" and testified in front of the

Texas State Senate Committee and House of Representatives multiple times in favor of Autism Education Bills.

Every Parent will have this hat on their Autism HatRack and wear it when the need arises to protect, inform and SUPPORT.

CHAPTER 9

## THE "SIBLING MIX"

*Our Three Blessings: Gregory, Jonathan & Danielle*

*The siblings to these amazing children with autism are heroes that make up the "Sibling Mix". They are earth angels who have witnessed pain, judgment, and rejection for themselves and their beloved brother or sister but will protect their siblings and be their voices. These amazing siblings have seen joy in challenging circumstances and understand empathy. The "Sibling Mix" will change the world.*

Gregory and Danielle were living lives with guidelines other kids never had to deal with. We didn't eat in restaurants all together for many years. David and I had to take turns going to the grocery store because we never knew what would trigger a "scream fest" from Jonathan, so it was easier to go without him. We had to forgo many family vacations due to finances being spent on therapies to help Jonathan and it was hard to change his surroundings.

Our family was a united group having to live in a divided environment. The kids would only have certain friends come over to play, who understood Jonathan's lack of language and weren't flustered by his hopping or squeals. It was so hard on the big kids to have to be "on alert" in their daily lives.

I always worried about Gregory and Danielle and if I was short changing them as a Mama because of all the attention Jonathan was getting, until a trip to Target (*yes, Target again*) clarified everything in the eyes of Jonathan's siblings.

I had gathered the courage to take all 3 kids to Target again because I needed to get a birthday gift for one of Gregory's friends. Target had the best price on Pokemon cards and Gregory wanted to pick them out. So we were going to do a dash into Target fast and with success. Once again, my "PMS Hat" was on!

We went into the store, I buckled Jonathan into the cart seat, landed Danielle into the main cart space and told Gregory to go to the Pokemon cards, we were right behind him. So far, everything was going according to plan. Jonathan was being great, Danielle was enjoying the cart ride and Gregory was surveying the Pokemon cards. We were in Target 5 minutes when our successful mission was coming to an end and we were at the checkout counter.

I was grabbing a Target gift card to add to the Pokemon packets Gregory had chosen, when Jonathan started to pull a Houdini and escape from his cart seat. I grabbed him right before he reached the end cap littered with DVD movies and plopped him back down into his cart seat and buckled him back up. I was grabbing my credit card and mentally pleading with the clerk to hurry and check me out, as Jonathan's howls started to reach the shrill level of glass shattering.

I ignored my son's screams (ABA techniques in action), as I maneuvered Danielle out of the cart, placed her to the left of me by Gregory, ready to head out of the store, but this time I was going to get my purchase. Jonathan was in the cart on my right, at the check out counter and for some reason, 2 packs of Pokemon cards and a gift card was taking FOREVER to ring up.

I was smiling to the clerk, as if I didn't hear the "scream-fest" to my right, and waited for her to punch in the Gift Certificate amount on our card but I could see that she was flustered. I felt terrible that my little crew was throwing a hiccup into her day, but I wasn't leaving with out the birthday gifts.

Then I saw a movement in my right peripheral vision. A man with a purposeful stride was coming in our direction. As I was waiting for my purchase, this man started jogging towards Jonathan and every warning bell was going off in my head. The man looked like he was high on drugs, with wild eyes and they were locked on Jonathan. I was still on the far side of the cart when I saw the man getting closer and then he raised his hand in the air as if to slap Jonathan in the face. I was trying to move the cart through the stall area to put myself between the man and Jonathan, but I wasn't fast enough. The man stopped his hand mid air and instead of hitting Jonathan, he leaned his face inches from Jonathan's face and screamed "SHUT UP!!"

I reached into the cart seat, snapped the strap open and grabbed Jonathan away from the man's reach. I shielded Jonathan with my body and in a low, cold voice, ordered the crazy man, "Get the hell away from my kid NOW!"

"Shut him up lady!" he was yelling at me as he was backing away. Then he turned and walked down the aisle as I stared holes into his back to make sure he didn't try and come after any of us again.

I was shaking and looked at the clerk and asked, "Are we finished here?"

She was shaking too and said, "Yes, you can sign on the tablet."

I still had Jonathan in my arms, but he had stopped howling by this point. The man had scared him so bad, that he was crying from fear, and his sobs were muffled into my chest. I said to the clerk, "I'm sorry about my son screaming and thank you for your help checking us out."

"No problem and I think that man is crazy." She said.

"I agree and you might want to get security, but we're leaving so don't worry about us." I asked Gregory to grab my purse and the Target bag, I reached for Danielle's hand and once again, asked God for the strength to get me through the Target electric doors.

We made it to the car and as I sat in my seat to take a deep breath, I looked into the rear view mirror at my children. Jonathan was still crying, but the volume was at a manageable level. Gregory was crying and it broke my heart. He never cried during "scream-fests", but he was at his breaking point and was saying it was his fault it happened because we had gone to Target for his Pokemon Cards.

I could not stop the ache coming deep from my heart for our older two children. A simple trip to Target had once again, gone to shit.

I was telling Gregory it wasn't his fault at all and that the man at Target was crazy, when Danielle asked, "Mama, why do we have Jonathan?"

I turned to see her beautiful blue eyes dry and clear. She wasn't crying but she had a furrow between her brows, as she asked such a direct question for a 6 year old.

"What do you mean, honey?" I asked grabbing tissues and passing them out.

"I mean, why do we have Jonathan? Why do we have to deal with him screaming all the time and being sad?"

It was one of those moments where I wanted to stop time. I knew that the answer to this innocent question was going to formulate in our children's minds for a lifetime. My answer had to be wise but simple. I took a deep breath and replied,

"Well, because if someone like the screaming man, inside the store, was raising Jonathan, then he wouldn't love him as much as we do and he wouldn't take care of him like we do. Does that help you with the 'why we have Jonathan'?"

"Yes." Danielle answered then kept talking, "I think it is because God wants us to love Jonathan even more than other people can." And there it was. From the mouth of our daughter, the love declared for her little brother.

"But Mama," Gregory was saying as he was trying to control his feelings, "Why does it have to be so hard. It's not fair."

"You're right. It is hard and it isn't fair. What you need to remember is that when things get hard for you, they are even harder for Jonathan. Jonathan can't "find his words" sometimes to ask for things he wants. Jonathan doesn't have any friends like you two do. Jonathan doesn't get asked to birthday parties like the one you are going to today. So when sad things happen, you really need to think of all the great stuff you two get to do, but Jonathan may never do."

I paused and looked at all three of our beautiful blessings and the tears had stopped. "Jonathan is teaching us things and we may not like all of the lessons we are having to learn, but we love him more than any other family could in the world."

Gregory and Danielle smiled and then Danielle asked, "Mama? Can we not take Jonathan to Target anymore. I just don't think he likes it there."

What a wise little girl we had. "I think you are right Danielle," and that was the last trip Jonathan made to Target for about a year.

CHAPTER 10

## THE SCHOOL ADVENTURES

*"In any moment of decision, the best thing you can do is the right thing. The worst thing you can do is nothing."*
- THEODORE ROOSEVELT

In August 2003, Jonathan turned 3 and aged out of ECI. We were really sad to see him move on from the therapists, but he was starting his adventure into Special Education Preschool (PPCD) in our school district and I was excited to have Jonathan in a preschool environment with Special Education trained teachers. Wow, was I naive.

We were putting our child into a brand new environment that didn't know his language, his "hiccups" or what triggered a "scream-fest". The school was set up with a PPCD room just for kids with special needs for a half-day program, so we were optimistic. We had our introduction into Special Education with an ARD (Admissions, Review and Dismissal) Meeting where we walked into a room expecting the PPCD teacher, Principal and the School's Diagnostician, but instead 7 adults with some smiles and some bored looks greeted us. I was intimidated at once trying to figure out who all these people were and why they were at the meeting.

The Diagnostician led the meeting with the Principal guiding responses from each teacher or therapist. We were handed a packet at least 20 pages thick with the words Individualized Education Program (IEP) across the top.

*I had no idea at that moment how important our child's IEP was going to be for his education, safety and legal rights, but you need to know it is your child's lifeline in the public schools.*

The meeting was very professional and laid out the next year of Jonathan's academic goals, social goals, schedule, and teacher ratio. In the meeting we agreed to an evaluation from the District Psychologist and cognitive testing to see where Jonathan's cognitive abilities were in comparison to other 3 years olds. All said and done, a very intimidating ARD ended up comforting David and me and we were really excited about starting PPCD for Jonathan. We were told the teacher had Special Education experience, a Special Needs Aide would be in the classroom to help and that there would be 5 children in his class.

Jonathan started his formal public education one week before his 3rd birthday and for the first few months, his half day program was a good experience, until I got a call from the Principal one afternoon at 4:00 pm, informing me that Jonathan's teacher had "lost" Jonathan for 30 minutes that day.

I was confused. I said I didn't understand what she was saying. I had picked Jonathan up from school at 11:30 am that day and no one told me Jonathan had been "lost". The Principal proceeded to tell me that at morning recess, Jonathan had disappeared from the playground where PPCD was interacting and playing with the regular ed Preschool kids. His teacher could not find him for 30 minutes, then someone called the school to report a child unaccompanied at a local neighborhood playground 1/4 mile away from the school and they found him there.

WHAT?!?!?!? I was so shocked at what the Principal was telling me, all I could ask was, "What? My limited-verbal, 3 year old child was lost at school and he ran by himself to a neighborhood playground through streets and cars and people and WHAT?"

The Principal was very calm and she continued on "Miss Victoria feels really bad about the whole thing and she is writing up a report that we will put in Jonathan's file about the incident."

Incident? Why the hell didn't they tell me what happened when they were smiling at me as they handed my son back to me that morning at 11:30. They never said a word and that was so screwed up. I was remembering how the teacher's aide had walked all the kids out from the school to the Moms waiting in their cars and I always got out to greet Jonathan on the sidewalk. The aide didn't say anything about "losing" Jonathan only an hour before. I asked how his day went and she gave me the regular answer of, "it was good and he ate his snack" response.

I told the Principal I still didn't understand how these events could have taken place.

She replied, "Miss Victoria is right here in my office and she wants to talk to you."

The Principal handed the phone to Victoria who got on the line with me and said, "Mrs. Bordelon, I am so sorry. We were out in the playground and when it was time to come back inside, I couldn't find Jonathan. We looked everywhere and then we found him at the playground located in the neighborhood."

"What happened Victoria? How did you lose him? Weren't you watching him?"

"Yes, we were all there, but you know how he likes to run, so I guess he remembered the other playground in the neighborhood and ran to it. I feel terrible and I am so sorry."

I remember being disgusted with her for a moment in time. I couldn't comprehend how she could endanger our son when I trusted her and the school. I felt deceived with their procedures when they saw me today after they had "lost" our son and didn't even tell me about the events. But what I despised the most was that the school, teacher and teacher's aide tried to cover up endangering our son because they knew Jonathan couldn't tell me what had happened at school that day.

Victoria and I hung up with her promising this would never happen again and she would write up a report to put in Jonathan's file. That night, I got a call from another Mom I knew from the afternoon PPCD class. She told me that she was the person who had seen Jonathan at the neighborhood playground that morning all alone. She knew he was supposed to be in PPCD, so she got worried and called the school.

A clarity bell went off in my head. That is why the Principal called me to tell me about what happened. She knew the other Mom who had found Jonathan at the playground would eventually call me and tell me what happened, so they had to cover their asses.

My rose-colored glasses came off after that experience with our public PPCD class that year. We ended up withdrawing Jonathan from PPCD and I finally found a private preschool, Apple Creek, which accepted Jonathan as a student if we hired a trained Shadow/Aide to attend preschool with him. We had Danielle enrolled at Apple Creek also, and we were spending lots of money, but we were seeing progress in Jonathan's social skills and compliance.

After a year of private preschool, a $20/hr shadow aide, private Speech and OT therapies, and medical expenses, we were having to look at public school again, but this time I was prepared. We enrolled Jonathan back into PPCD at the same school, but we requested he go back into the system to repeat the first year of PPCD. His social skills were that of a 2 year old, so I was hoping being with other 3-4 year olds, not 4-5 year olds would be more beneficial. The teacher that year was kind and calm-the best mix for Jonathan. We had a successful PPCD experience for the next 2 years. We had hiccups, but to the best of my knowledge, they never "lost" our son during school time again.

After a few more rounds of enrolling Jonathan into public school, withdrawing him to attend an ABA learning Center, and then enrolling him again the next year, it was truly a shuffle of schools. We stayed in our School District's Special Needs program for 6 years. There were roller coaster moments, good teachers and bad. But our main objective was to have Jonathan learn academic and social skills alongside his neurotypical peers. Every summer we would have progression from Jonathan and he would be doing great for the first half of the school year. Then after Christmas, he would start to regress and not achieve any IEP goals. This was a pattern for most of the 6 years we were in Public school, but he loved going to school and the interaction. Jonathan was verbal now, compliant, and attending his mainstream classes 50% of his day. We were very proud of him.

*Public schools are tricky and my feelings are mixed. We live in a school district with exemplary schools and award winning teachers. Still to this day if anyone asks me about our school district I tell them, I am the biggest fan of our District's Regular Education. Gregory and Danielle excelled in the school district with the help and guidance of wonderful, caring teachers who nurtured their minds and interests.*

*Gregory started in 2nd grade and went on to the High School to graduate at the top 9% of his class, he helped run the new Broadcast studio, he was involved in volunteer organizations and was even crowned Homecoming King his Senior year by his peers.*

*Danielle loved grade school and started middle school with AP academics, engaged in Robotics and won a state championship. She started playing the violin and joined the orchestra. The Orchestra*

*Director was an earth angel for our little girl as she ignited her love for music that will be a lifelong adventure for her.*

Our school district's Regular Education program was great, but when you ask me about Special Needs Education, the truth is:

Your child's experience and safety depends on his or her teacher and the Principal of the school. Period. You could be in the best school district in America, but if you have a teacher that doesn't follow your child's IEP or comes to school with a hangover and doesn't have the patience and experience to educate your child that day, your child suffers. And more times than not, the Principal will help cover it up.

We found out the hard way on March 10, 2010…but that was also the day God wasn't silent anymore in my life.

CHAPTER 11

## GOD WASN'T SILENT ANYMORE

*"All who call on God in true faith, earnestly from the heart, will certainly be heard, and will receive what they have asked and desired."*
- MARTIN LUTHER

Our family was 9 years into Jonathan's life journey twisted with the challenges of autism. We had years of different therapies under our belt and some had proven helpful and beneficial to his healing. Jonathan was emerging from his autism bubble and he would sneak in these "one liner" responses that would make us laugh and confirm his mind was trying to clear away the fog. It was wonderful to see a sense of humor from him and a twinkle in his eyes.

The summer before his 2$^{nd}$ grade year at school, Jonathan's language was progressing and he was having conversations that led to more and more interaction with peers and his siblings. His anxieties were at an all time low and we were so positive he would have a great year in school, the ARD committee (that included the school administration team and the parents) set his schedule up for 4 hours mainstream classes and 2 hour Special Needs classroom support a day. Jonathan was becoming a success story and we were thrilled.

Life at home was going great and all the kids were thriving. I had been wearing my PMS Hat for years by this time and found it worked. I opened my line of communication with God more and more with gratitude for the healing taking place within our family and I was reaching out helping other families going through the autism journey.

Things were on a forward path for Jonathan and he was even given a speaking part in the Thanksgiving classroom play his Regular Education teacher was directing. We were so proud to see him next to his 2nd grade peers, reading his lines and performing his role. Jonathan had never been included in a school performance before, and he was amazing.

It was after Thanksgiving break that things started to go wrong. Jonathan started to tell us "No more school" or "No Miss Teacher" *(I refuse to write his Special Education Teacher's name in my book and you will soon find out why).* I had contacted his teacher to have a meeting to discuss his reluctance to go to school, because it wasn't normal. We had a meeting and Miss Teacher told me Jonathan was doing great and that she didn't know why he was saying those things.

This was the first of many, *she is not telling me the truth*, feelings I started to get from his teacher. I was always alarmed to hear the words "I don't know" from a Special Needs Teacher responsible for our "extra needs" son. "I don't know" was unacceptable in my eyes because there is always, ALWAYS, a reason for a child's actions and manners and as a Special Needs Teacher- you are suppose to know. Jonathan continued to have anxieties going to school, but because the teacher was telling us everything was fine at school, we couldn't pinpoint his anxieties for going to school, because he couldn't define them to us.

Jonathan's language started to regress. His behaviors started to get worse at school. He would have a melt down when he had to take a shower at home, which used to be one of his favorite things to do at the end of a long day. He would freak out when I would try and towel him dry, and start screaming video script titles at me that didn't make any sense.

We were losing Jonathan back to his autism bubble and it was terrible. I was feeling hopeless again trying to figure things out and why he was so scared of school and every night when Jonathan would say his nighttime prayers, he would end it with "No school tomorrow".

We would tell him that he did have school tomorrow, but we would count the week with him to help with his anxiety about school. I would say to him, "Yes we have school because tomorrow is Marvelous Monday, then Terrific Tuesday, Wonderful Wednesday, Thrilling Thursday, Fabulous Friday, then Super Saturday & Sunday". This went on every night for weeks.

David and I called an emergency ARD committee meeting to go over Jonathan's IEP, daily schedule and expectations to see if we needed to change anything to make it less stressful. The Teacher and Principal seemed unconcerned about Jonathan's changes and kept telling us that nothing was different at school. None of it made sense.

On January 13, 2010, I got a call from the school Nurse. She told me Jonathan had an accident on the swing in the DEAR (his Special Needs) Classroom and she had cleaned him up but he seemed to still be hurt. I told her I was on my way and got to the school to find Jonathan laying down on the Nurse's office cot whining. Miss Teacher was sitting on the edge of the cot and I asked her what happened.

"Well Mom, somebody got a little too high on the swing and hurt his back." She replied and moved off the cot so I could sit next to Jonathan who curled up into my lap and I pulled up his shirt to see his back and gasped. Jonathan had an abrasion 9 inches long down the length of his spine. It had turned purple and blue and blood pricks were coming to the surface. He had skin scraped off on the edges and as I looked at his teacher who was standing there I asked again, "What happened and what did he scrape his back on?"

"I don't know" was her answer yet again. She continued to explain, "I didn't see it happen, but I think he hit the bookcase. All I know is I heard him start crying and saying 'poor Jonathan' and put his hand on his back. I saw he hurt himself and brought him down to Nurse J."

I knew Miss Teacher was lying. She kept looking away from my eyes as she was telling her tale and I didn't know what part of her story she was lying about, but I knew she was lying. This was becoming a constant level of her communication. The problem now was my son was hurt and I didn't want to use any more pretenses with this woman who was letting our son get hurt.

"You have got to be kidding me. Who was in the room and saw what happened? Wasn't anyone watching him?" I asked while still holding Jonathan in my lap.

"No. No one saw what happened" she was sticking with her story and her tone was getting snippy.

I looked at Nurse J who had been sitting there and I was so grateful she had called me about Jonathan's injury. I asked what time this had happened and they both looked at each other before answering. Then his teacher said "About 10:00 am."

I looked at her stunned. Nurse J had called me this afternoon to tell me he had hurt his back, but he had been injured hours ago. The nurse interjected and said, "Maureen, I cleaned his back up earlier and applied ice for the swelling. He seemed fine but then I think his shirt started to irritate him so that was when I called you."

"Thank you Nurse J", I said and I meant it. I thought, my God, the teacher didn't even call me, but the Nurse did. I wanted to get Jonathan out of there before I had to hear any more lies coming from Miss Teacher. I asked Nurse J to please make a report of the accident and I took Jonathan home.

Two weeks later I got another call from Nurse J at school that Jonathan had fallen, yet again, from the swing and he had knocked his head on the tile floor hard. I raced up to the school and he had a goose egg the size of a golf ball at the base of his skull. I asked Nurse J if she had checked him for a concussion and she said she checked but did not see signs of a concussion. I left and went right to Jonathan's doctor to have him double-checked and look at his eyes and head. We monitored him for sleepiness, vomiting and headaches for the next 24 hours.

This was crazy, Jonathan was getting hurt in his classroom and the only one who seemed to care was the Nurse. Jonathan couldn't tell me what was happening in his classroom and his teacher was taking advantage of his silence. David and I called a meeting with the Principal and didn't return Jonathan to school until we had the meeting. It took two days, but we met and David and I requested a new teacher for Jonathan immediately. The environment of his classroom was not safe and he needed a teacher who "did know" what was going on.

His teacher was in the meeting and I had no problem telling her that her "I don't knows" were unacceptable. We requested Jonathan transferred to another Resource teacher in the school and put the plan in place for an observation trail the next week. We were satisfied with the new transition promises and returned Jonathan back to school to move forward with the new teacher. My last thoughts leaving the meeting with the Principal and his teacher was I knew Jonathan would be in his teacher's care for a few more days, but she wouldn't dare let him get hurt on the swing again…and he didn't get hurt on the swing, it was much, much worse.

On March 10, 2010, Jonathan was abused, restrained by his teachers and then confined to a padded blue cell inducing him to vomit in his special needs classroom at school. His teacher called me and her words chilled me to the bone. "Jonathan is really upset and he won't calm down. I don't know what to do. I've tried everything, even the towel." I was baffled. I had just been up at the school 40 minutes earlier to observe Jonathan in a new classroom setting with a new teacher we were transitioning him to, and when I left, he was fine. He was walking back to his Special Needs/DEAR classroom with Miss Teacher happy and compliant; and what was she talking about "the towel"?

"What happened?" I demanded.

Miss Teacher replied, "He wouldn't get off the computer so he started throwing a fit and he hit me." The problem with this is now, she was telling me he was hitting her and she didn't know what to do. It was no use trying to breakdown the reasoning, because the teacher had been untrustworthy about what was happening in the classroom, so I said, "Do you want me to talk to him?"

"Yes" was her curt reply.

It was then I could hear crying and harsh coughing in the background. His teacher muffled the phone and I could hear her talk to someone but I couldn't make out her words. She came back on the line. "He can't come to the phone. He is throwing up".

"What?!?" I yelled, "You got him so upset that he is throwing up?"

Then she said something so ridiculous I couldn't believe it. "It's your fault Mom. He was upset seeing you at school this morning".

Now, that was just bullshit. He was fine when I left him in her "capable hands" 40 minutes ago. At that point, I knew I had to go get him away from Miss Teacher. She was in no condition to educate him and her hostile, angry words were evidence to me that she was out of control in her classroom. I couldn't even image what she had done to make Jonathan so upset that he was throwing up.

I responded in a low-tone, terse voice, "I'm coming to get him."

I drove up to the school and found the school's front desk clerk standing at the school doors.

She opened the door and greeted me, "Hi Mrs. Bordelon, how are you today?"

I was a little taken aback as to why she was greeting me at the door, since that had never happened before, but I replied, "I'm fine but Jonathan isn't. I'm here to pick him up."

She ushered me into the school and there was another lady behind the front desk. I asked her to call down to Jonathan's classroom and tell Miss Teacher I was here to get Jonathan. To my surprise the lady behind the desk said, "Oh, he is in Nurse J's clinic."

I remember thinking, "Wow, that was fast", as I walked into the main office where Nurse J's clinic was located. I moved past the Teacher's Aide's 250 lb frame, who was blocking the doorway and I saw my baby boy. His face was bright red, and he was walking fast in circles, hitting his chest with his hand and gasping for breath. I looked at his tear stained face and watery eyes and yelled, "Oh my God, Jonathan, are you choking?"

Jonathan turned and saw me, and for a brief moment there was relief in his face and with a raspy voice he replied, "YES"!

He went to the sink and started to dry heave whatever was stuck in his throat. I raced to him and performed the Heimlich while the school staff just watched. He threw up a few spit-fulls of mucus, but his anxiety was off the charts and he couldn't stop his body from dry heaving. I needed him to calm his body, which would relax his sternum and esophagus so he could dislodge whatever was stuck.

I looked over at the Teacher's Aide and asked, "What is he choking on?"

"I don't know" she replied. "He had his apple snack but then he threw up and we thought he was all done."

"Done with what?" I asked totally shocked that she wasn't performing the Heimlich on him to help him dislodge the apple.

"Done with throwing up." She answered.

I was pissed. Her nonchalant attitude was disturbing. "Why didn't you help him? Can't you see he is choking on something? Don't you know the Heimlich maneuver?"

"No and I would never touch him that way." That was her answer which totally translated into: No Mom, I will watch your son choke before I try and help him. Well, that was obvious.

(*I uncovered after this terrible day: The Special Needs Teacher and 2 aides in charge of 6 limited verbal autistic boys were NOT trained in CPR or Heimlich emergency maneuvers. They got certified 2 weeks <u>after our son's incident</u>.*)

I turned to Jonathan and applied short, brisk, upward strokes to his back to help dislodge the apple. Then I did the Heimlich on him and Nurse J tried to get Jonathan to sip water between applications to help force the apple down his esophagus. This went on for 10 more minutes and Jonathan kept whispering "home", so after he caught his breath, we left the school and raced home.

He still wasn't getting a full, deep breath so I knew whatever was stuck, was still lodged inside. On the way home I even thought to go to the fire department in the neighborhood, but Jonathan's anxieties were so high, I was afraid a strange, big firemen trying to perform the Heimlich would terrify him and make things worse. We pulled into the garage and Jonathan raced into the kitchen and leaned over the sink to try and dislodge the apple and dry heave. I ran behind him and quickly started to say calming, loving words and rubbing his back to help calm his convulsing body.

He was gasping for gulps of air and I knew I had to apply some backstrokes hard to loosen up whatever was caught in his throat.

"Honey, Mama is going to stroke you on the back to help get your apple free, OK?" I wanted him to know the jolt was coming.

Jonathan couldn't speak anymore; his face was past red and was now getting purple. He just looked at me with trusting eyes and nodded his head. I applied two hard upwards strokes on his back to help loosen the lodged apple and nothing happened. I turned my head to look for my phone to call 911 and Jonathan leaned back into me and went limp.

"Jonathan!" I screamed, "Honey, can you hear me?" no response from my beautiful, angel boy.

Jonathan was slumped in my arms as I had his 65-pound body pressed to the sink counter so he wouldn't fall to the ground. I couldn't let him go.

I started screaming "Jonathan, I'm here honey, don't die, breath, spit, Jonathan!"

No response. It was THE MOST HELPLESS moment of my life. My son was dying in my arms. The only thought I had was pure horror and desperation of needing help. This was out of my hands and I couldn't fix him!

Tears started rolling down my face, blurring my vision and I had this guttural scream emit from my body.

"God- HELP ME!!! Where are you? He is dying and he can't breath! Don't let him die"

I looked up to the ceiling and screamed out to my Grandmother in heaven "Mimi- help me save him"

I looked to the right and yelled in the air to my husband's Uncle, who had passed away and gone to heaven. "Don -help me! You love Jonathan! Don't take him from me now Damn it!"

"God, Mimi, Don - HELP ME! I NEED YOU NOW!!!"

Then I lifted Jonathan up and laid him over the sink and said,

"Baby, I am going to try this one more time and it might hurt. But Mama is going to try and push the apple out from your throat" Jonathan wasn't responding, he was purple and limp and I knew that if I didn't get the apple out he was going to die. Jonathan was drifting away from me and I could feel his soul leaving my kitchen.

Then, I felt it and I knew I was not alone. God wasn't silent anymore. I could feel his presence and Mimi and Uncle Don's spirits in the kitchen by my sides. Just like I had always felt Mimi at certain times, this awareness of powerful forces were virtually a physical pressure surrounding Jonathan and me at the kitchen sink. I felt strength to not give up and keep trying.

While I had him leaning into the sink, I maneuvered my hands up under his rib cage and pressed into his stomach so hard I thought I was going to break him in half. I did an upturned- rotated pull into his gut and pushed up into his ribcage and his whole body lurched forward and Jonathan threw up a mouthful of mucus and a severed slice of green apple.

Jonathan took a HUGE deep breath and gulped air in. He was alive! His face drained from purple to bright red in seconds. He was taking his second deep breath and I felt such relief and gratitude. I turned him around and fell to my knees, crying and hugging him.

"Honey can you breath?" and his beautiful, bloodshot eyes looked into mine and he said in a raspy, soft voice "Better."

This was my day to recognize a miracle had happened and Jonathan was alive. God wasn't silent anymore. He was strong and merciful, and had given me our son back. He came when I needed him most and he filled my kitchen with a powerful aura of support. I remember the sun shining into the sink window onto Jonathan's purple, lifeless face and how in a moment of pure surrender to God, I found strength the moment I needed it most.

One week later we got Jonathan into the GI doctor for an endoscope surgery because I was so scared his esophagus was damaged, and I was right. The GI specialist, came out of the operating room, and said "I have no idea how that boy was eating solid foods. His esophagus is swollen shut and raw with ulcers. He is on a liquid diet starting now for at least 30 days."

We found out from the biopsies taken from the endoscopy that Jonathan had Eosinophilic Esophagitis (EE), chronic gastritis, severe allergies and reflux. All of these physical issues were only one part of Jonathan's suffering.

We had found out the truth of the teachers actions on that terrible morning at school. Miss Teacher and the Aide had constrained Jonathan by wrapping him with a beach towel, inciting his vomiting and choking, then threw him into a padded, blue seclusion room and trapped him in there until she called me.

The months following March 10, 2010, took me to such a negative, defensive, angry place in my life. The school had decided to circle their wagons and deny Jonathan a homebound education and wanted us to return Jonathan back into his traumatic, toxic environment at the school with the teacher who had restrained him, violated his IEP, and had neglected him. They were crazy!

As David and I had ARD meeting after ARD meeting following the education laws and supplying medical documentation of

Jonathan's illnesses, the administration kept denying Special Needs Homebound Education. When over a month had gone by with no education, David and I reminded the ARD committee of their purposeful withholding of Jonathan's education and they finally agreed to send a teacher to our home a few hours a week.

Then one afternoon, in May, the Special Education Coordinator for the District came to our home, unannounced with another District Coordinator and handed me a letter informing us that the school would have a lawyer to represent the District (with our tax dollars of course) to attend our next ARD meeting. As if this experience couldn't get any crazier, the bullies had left the classroom and now had come to our front door to intimidate us. That was when I knew the District had declared battle on our son's future education and our family. We didn't have money for a lawyer, and we needed help. David and I had been defending our stance of Jonathan's illness by ourselves, but I needed another miracle. We got one in the form of an angel Warrior Mom named Jennifer.

My brother-in-law knew a lawyer named Sarah, who was familiar to the world of autism and she met with me one Sunday morning and listened to our plight. Sarah's expertise was not in Special Ed Law, but she knew another Mom who might be able to help us. She forwarded my info to a woman named Jennifer who was involved with the Elizabeth Birt Center for Autism Law and Advocacy (EBCALA) and a kick butt Warrior Mom in Dallas.

Jennifer was our earth angel on Jonathan's Angel Team of healing. With the support of her local Law Firm and EBCALA, she took our case and for the next 9 months, Jennifer was at our side in ARD meetings, legal complaint filings with TEA, Due Process Hearings, a Civil lawsuit, Medical evaluations and Mediations.

We had requested Jonathan's school staff emails (as is every parent's legal rights) from the year 2009-2010 and were shocked at the documented contempt from the school personnel towards our family. There were shameless emails from Miss Teacher through out school year, disregarding Jonathan's safety and her disdain towards me. The Principal had written an email to Miss Teacher in regards to a parent –teacher meeting, where she wrote threats to me "the Mom" to "take me down". Unfortunately, they tried to take our defenseless, 9 year old son down instead while he was in their care.

At our request and filing, Texas Education Agency (TEA) court ordered deposition testimonies of involved school staff, taken on August 12, 2010. Under oath, the truth was revealed of neglect, restraint and illegal confinement done to Jonathan during the school year of 2009-2010.

I know without a doubt, that God, Mimi, Uncle Don and my posse of angels watched over Jonathan while he was in the hands of his teachers and helped me save his life that terrifying morning. I know the Universe had brought Jennifer into our lives and after 9 months of battles, sleepless nights, and a crash course in Special Education law (for the parents), we resolved Jonathan's case.

Jonathan never returned to school and is still healing from Post Traumatic Stress Disorder, EE, allergies and anxiety. I think of March 10, 2010, as a re-birth day for Jonathan and me. Every day is precious and seeing him happy and healing is my gift from God and my angels.

CHAPTER 12

## THE HEALING

*"Nothing is impossible; the word itself says 'I'm possible'!"*
- AUDREY HEPBURN

Where March 10, 2010, was the worst day of my life, I didn't want to feel like an injured party any more. I didn't want the school attached to us with the negative harm they had inflicted on Jonathan and our family. The only way I knew how to do that back then, was to focus on healing Jonathan with the targeted injuries from his ordeal.

Jonathan received an Independent Evaluation from a Dallas Child Psychologist who diagnosed Jonathan with severe anxieties and signs of Post Traumatic Stress Disorder (PTSD) from his ordeals at school. His GI doctor recommended keeping Jonathan's stress levels to a minimum as anxiety contributed to exasperate EE in the body, so we did by keeping him home.

He went on a strict liquid diet for the allotted 30 days and while on the diet, we did two types of allergy testing. One type was a medical IgG & IgE blood allergy tests to get a reading on what he was allergic to that was triggering his EE, gastritis, reflux and airborne allergies. The results took up to 3-4 weeks but I needed to know his immediate allergies right away.

So the second type of allergy testing we did was an alternative energy reading with one of our earth angels on Jonathan's healing team: Danette Goodyear. Danette was certified in *Electrodermal Screening (EDS)*[5], where we could read Jonathan's allergies through his body's energy. These results were immediate so I could adapt his environment around his sensitivities right away and build his immune system back up.

The results from both sets of allergy testing matched up and Jonathan's allergies had changed through the years with his development. He was even more sensitive to dust mites, corn, nuts, alcohol, chalk dust, synthetic carpet, cedar wood, and a list of other antigens that most all existed in the walls of the schools: plastics, carpets, cleaning supplies, dry erase boards and even the playground.

So I knew we had to treat his allergies, but due to the severity of his reactions, we couldn't treat his allergies in a mainstream fashion, so I investigated energy allergy treatments and we started Nambudripad's Allergy Elimination Techniques (NAET)[6] right away. Within a few treatments we saw positive results with NAET.

I then started to build Jonathan's immune system with Young Living therapeutic grade Essential Oils[7]. The YLEOs were our medicine and allergy treatments. Where NAET would clear Jonathan's sensitivities to things, the YLEOs would help repair and build his immune system naturally on a cellular level, so he could strengthen his body and heal his EE, gut, inflammation, brain and more.

We didn't really know how to approach the PTSD. When we took Jonathan to his Psychiatrist, I was told that as his Mother, I would know how Jonathan was feeling, better than anyone else trying to interpret his emotions. So, I concentrated on keeping Jonathan calm, feeling safe and secure within his environment. We had to rebuild his self-esteem and lessen his fears.

---

[5] See Chapter 17 - EDS
[6] See Chapter 17 - NAET
[7] See Chapter 19-My "Essential Oils Hat"

This took years, but I knew I was making progress when I was making a video of Jonathan 7 months after that terrible March morning. We were recording Jonathan's math-counting session and our brave, beautiful son told me how he was scared of school and his teacher because she threw him into the "Blue room" (which was the padded cell-room) inside his classroom. After he started to tell me his fears, we worked on reassuring his safety and letting him know he was never going back to see Miss Teacher and that classroom again.

*Of course cameras in ALL the public special needs classrooms would eliminate any future tragedies: Parents are working on passing legislative bills in states across the country.*
*A great Facebook group with current information is:*
*https://www.facebook.com/CamerasInSpecialNeedsClassrooms*

In the months that passed, Jonathan taught me his video scripting language[8] and how he was using video titles and the lessons of the movies, as his way to communicate. I spent months with my "Decoding Hat" on translating the meaning of his videos into every day language that would eventually help build his communication. He was healing more and more. Jonathan was slowly coming back out of his autism bubble and into our lives again.

I was elated and exhausted. I had targeted physical issues I could help Jonathan heal from and connected with him emotionally to rebuild his self-esteem. I finally had a communication tool that helped me break through the barriers of language he had built up around him.

Jonathan was flourishing and started to show signs of healing. Gone were the days of separate vacations, outings and adventures. Jonathan wanted to see movies in a movie theater, play with other

---

[8] Talking in Videos…an Autism Language - www.MyAutismHatRack.com

children, surf in the ocean and his anxieties were lessening. He was engaging again and wanted to go on adventures with us.

His relationships with everyone started to blossom and on many days we felt like a "normal family" with the absence of any autism challenges.

Before I knew it, 2 years had gone by and while our youngest son was healing and in turn, helping our whole family heal, our oldest son was preparing to leave the nest for his own adventure in life…and God was preparing me for another "Life Flip".

CHAPTER 13

## THE MISSING PIECE OF THE PUZZLE

*"A mind, once stretched by a new idea,
never regains its original dimensions."*
- OLIVER WENDELL HOLMES

I was a Warrior Mama, doing my job and healing our youngest son, but now, I was facing sending our oldest son into the world outside my reach. I didn't want to feel the melancholy I was experiencing with Gregory leaving the nest. I had done my job and help raise an amazing young man ready to take on the world and I wanted him to fly!

David knew I was starting to get gloomy even before I did. He suggested I take the two big kids on a trip to California and go look at colleges for Gregory and spend some time with my Dad in San Diego. Jonathan was in a good place and the break was very tempting for me, so we made plans to visit 3 different California Universities, see my Dad & his wife Jeannie, visit some friends and hit Comic Con for Danielle in an 8-day adventure.

It was the best trip I had been on in years and by the end of it, Gregory had chosen his future college and Danielle had her mind blown away and dreams attained by meeting Manga Artists and Comic Con gurus. We all had a great visit with my Dad and Jeannie, our wonderful friends who had moved to California, and we touched our toes in the sand of 4 major beaches down the Pacific Coast

Highway. I loved spending time with our oldest kids and cherished every moment.

We were taking our last morning stroll on Manhattan Beach and Gregory and I were walking along the surf, Danielle was reading her book on a blanket a few yards away and the weather was perfect. Gregory threw his arm over my shoulder as we looked out to the ocean at the surfers catching their waves, and he casually said,

"Well Mama, it's your turn."

I smiled up at him, as he had passed me in height a few years back, and said, "What do you mean, 'my turn'?"

"It's your turn to start working on you. You've made Jonathan better, Danielle is doing great, Papa is good and I'm about to have the best senior school year ever. You've taken care of all of us and now it's your turn to do your thing?"

I laughed and said, "Oh Gregory, I love you. You guys ARE "my thing".

He smiled and said, "I know Mama, but it's your turn for you, not us."

And at that moment of clarity, with my oldest child wisely telling me, to think about myself and not him, Danielle, Jonathan or David, but me, I realized he was giving me the green light to move forward. I didn't even know I needed it, but I did.

I had been so busy for the past 17+ years raising, healing, caring, and supporting everyone I loved, because I wanted to. It gave me a mission and a purpose, but I lost me in the daily shuffle and I was running on fumes very close to empty. I promised myself that day that I would "find my thing" and "take my turn" and I said a prayer to Mimi asking for guidance and signs to help me along the way. I couldn't help but laugh at the thought running through my head, as we walked from the surf towards Danielle on her blanket, that the missing piece of the puzzle I had been searching for all these years was...ME.

Guidance came a little over a year later in the form of a posse of angels, a push on a sidewalk and the numbers 333.

---

Gregory had applied and been accepted to the University of Texas in Austin and Chapman University in Orange, California. Of course we were hoping to have his college commute only 3 hours away by car, but his heart was set on Chapman and his hard earned scholarships came through to make it possible. In August of 2012, all 5 of us took him to college so we could envision where Gregory's next chapter was beginning. The last thing we wanted for Jonathan was not to know where Gregory was going and to think he had just disappeared. We ALL needed the visuals of where he would be.

It was so hard to say goodbye and leave Gregory at Chapman, but knowing he was at the right University and he was starting his life path, not just continuing his education, made the heartache a little easier.

A few months later, David had surprised me with a ticket for our Anniversary to go out and see Gregory for Parent's weekend. It was the best Anniversary gift he could have given me.

On October 5, I flew into John Wayne Airport, 20 minutes from the Chapman campus. I had price lined a great rate at a 4-star hotel and decided to check into my room before going to get Gregory. At check-in, the hotel desk clerk handed me my room key and I glanced down and saw the numbers 333. I smiled and joked with her saying,

"I sure will remember those number easily, I have 3 kids." I went to my room, freshened up and headed to go see our oldest baby.

Gregory was coming out of his dorm as I pulled up to the curb, parked and jumped out of the car to surprise him and it was one of my favorite moments in life. After 18 years of getting to hug your kid almost every day, not being able to see him for 2 months was too long and I swear I must have hugged him for 5 whole minutes.

I was so happy! I was happy because he looked great, he loved school, the people and he was happy. We decided to head to Newport to go eat an early dinner and off we went. One of the things I love to do when we travel is eat at local dining spots. I don't like chain restaurants because I can eat at those back home. So we were driving along the Pacific highway and there were a couple of chain restaurants, so we passed them by. I took a right at the next street and there was a restaurant that I hadn't heard of and a "free valet" sign in the parking lot –*SOLD* and I pulled right in!

We went inside and it was a charming restaurant right on the marina. Gregory was catching me up on all his activities about school, a fraternity he had joined, and his campus job in Admissions. I was absorbed and living in the moment, enjoying every detail of Gregory's adventures.

We left the restaurant to head back to campus and Gregory asked me,

"Mama, what was the name of the restaurant we were at so I can tell my friends we need to come back here?" We were stopped at a red light and I turned around to read the name of the restaurant.

"3- Thirty-Three. *Oh my God!*"

"What is it?" Gregory had stopped typing the restaurant name into his phone.

"That's the number of my hotel room. And look at the numbers on that pole: 333" I was floored. "That is so weird, right?"

I turned back around to look at Gregory and he shrugged his shoulders and said, "Uh, ok, I guess so." not impressed

I thought it was really weird. The light turned green and we headed back to campus and the numbers 333 took a back seat in my head. The rest of the night was fun as Gregory and I strolled the college town of Orange, met some of his friends and just enjoyed each other's company.

The next morning I had an appointment with a Reiki Master for a Vibrational Alignment. My girlfriend Nathalie had introduced me to Tami Duncan, who had recovered her son from Lyme Induced Autism (LIA), herself from Lyme disease and founded the LIA Foundation. She had done an Autism Intuitive Balancing on Jonathan long distance a few weeks ago and her office was so close to Orange, I wanted to have a healing session with her in person. I dragged Gregory along with me, and as I went into Tami's office for our session, Gregory found a comfortable place on her couch and was asleep in minutes.

I instantly liked Tami. Her energy was positive and open. She made me feel at ease and as she was using her special methods of healing with sound bowls, channeling spirit and connecting with my aura, her message for me was "Let it go". I was worrying too much, taking on too much stress and trying to control things that were out of my control. I joked with her that she had just defined the textbook definition of every Mother raising a child with autism, and she agreed, but for me to heal, I needed to "Let it go".

My first thought was "Let which things go?" so I asked Tami and she replied I needed to let go of the guilt I was carrying around, blame, anger, and sadness. I needed to let go of trying to control autism and take a rest.

Now I thought I had done a pretty good job of staying positive and letting go of my anger towards autism. Tami's reply struck a cord with me. She said I was still trying to control Jonathan's recovery, when I needed to release the control, set the path and let God, his angels and my spirit guides lead the way.

Honestly, I had no idea how to do that. In my head, her words translated as me giving up on our son ever fully recovering from autism's ailments, but she was assuring me just the opposite and reiterating: "Let it go".

*I believe God understood my inner plight because the weeks that followed, Mimi-isms and opportunities presented themselves in such a way that I could "let go" and then more healing began.*

I left the session with what I could only describe as being "lighthearted". She had cut cords of negative bindings from me that were deep and I felt lighter. I didn't know if it was because I was in California and away from my every day stresses, but there was no denying, I was feeling "lighter and carefree".

Gregory and I headed back to Chapman for a BBQ his fraternity was holding for all the parents. We found a parking spot a couple of blocks away and started walking along the sidewalk that ran down the length of the town.

We were passing a cute antique shop when all of the sudden, I felt this huge push on my left shoulder and I was going down! I gasped and reached out to grab Gregory's arm to stop my fall. Gregory reacted and grabbed me before I hit the pavement and when I straightened up, I was still feeling pulled to the ground. I wasn't dizzy and I hadn't tripped, but I was pushed.

"Mama, what happened?" Gregory asked concerned.

"I don't know. I was pushed." Was all I could explain.

"Mama, no one is around." And he was right.

I still was trying to straighten up because an undetectable pressure of force was still around me. The pressure reminded me of that morning at the kitchen sink with Jonathan, but none of that made sense to me.

I had a death grip on Gregory's right arm when I looked over his shoulder and saw IT. I gasped again and Gregory said "What?"

He was getting irritated thinking I was playing some sort of game, and all I could say was, "Look!" and pointed across the street at a University Campus Building. Exactly lined up to us from across the street, was a building marked with big, bold numbers: 333.

"Ok, now Mama, that is weird." He said very quietly.

"Gregory, that is more than weird, that is a sign and someone or something just pushed me to make sure we saw it." I took a couple of deep breaths and finally felt the pressure fade and I got my footing solid again. We continued on our walk to the BBQ a few blocks down, but I was walking like a turtle afraid I was going to get pushed again.

I didn't know what to make about the numbers. 333: three times in 24 hours and it was obviously a strong sign and Mimi-ism. What did it mean? Was something going to happen at 3:33 pm? 3:33 am? On March 3, 2013? I could do hundreds of scenarios but how would I know what the answer was? I was beginning to think my Rheki Healing earlier that morning had "opened" me up to a force I had been keeping at arms length...God.

The next day, I headed back to Dallas and I did not have any more "pushes" or notice any more 333's after I had checked out of the hotel. But when I landed back home and in the following weeks, I had more "Mimi-isms" and signs get my attention, than I had ever experienced in my life.

The Universe was aligning and presenting to me, my Divine Pathway. I had taken the steps to let go of trying to control things that were "out of my control". I was willing to forgive autism, vaccines, Jonathan's teachers and all the baggage with it. And finally, I was working on releasing my fears for Jonathan's future.

That Tuesday, I took Jonathan to his weekly OT appointment with another earth angel on Jonathan's healing team, Betsy Williams. I told her about the #333 occurrences and she agreed with me that there was a meaning behind the numbers, but we couldn't figure it out. A few days later, Betsy sent me a text with an attachment that that read, "Check out the number 333" and there was an article attached written by a lady named Doreen Virtue, PhD.

The article was about *Angel Numbers 101*, and the meanings behind the numbers are signs from your angels, God and the universe. I looked up 333 and it read:

*"You are completely surrounded, protected, loved and guided by the benevolent ascended masters."* It continued to identify the ascended masters as: Mother Mary, Jesus, Moses, Archangel Michael, Archangel Raphael, and more.

That was a heavy hitting list of angels and saints, and in those few seconds, I had a full body chill run through my core and a certainty of knowing that I had a posse of angels by my side. Snippets of exasperated, memories flew through my mind: the "Moses Moment" at Target and the sea of people parted so I could get my children to the electric doors and home.

That day in our kitchen when I surrendered to God and called out for help and he had spared Jonathan's life. I knew I had God, Mimi and Don by my side. And now, literally getting a "PUSH" and knocked over with a clear sign of the #333 on a room key, restaurant and a building, I was ready to pay attention and quit putting God at arms length. I was ready to ask for help and guidance to a realm I had not *totally surrendered* to in regards to my world of Autism.

A week later, I told my girlfriend Carolyn my story about the #333. She had heard about Doreen Virtue and had a few of her CDs and books. When we met up for lunch, Carolyn had gone and bought me Doreen Virtue's <u>The Lightworker's Way</u> book as a gift. This was not a book I would have bought myself. Why? Because for 12+ years, most non-fiction books I had read were about Autism and not about God or connecting to Angels.

<u>The Lightworker's Way</u> resonated with me like no other "self help" book had. Doreen Virtue wrote about her spirituality connecting with Angels and God. The way she explained that the Angels are God's loving messengers, nondenominational and always there to help when called upon, helped me connect on a spiritual level that I had been grasping for. It made sense to me along my thought process from my younger days at the hospital as to why Blaine, Tessa and Kathleen all had died so young. They had gone to heaven to be with God and I attributed their souls as angels watching over me my whole life.

Reading through her book, there were topics I needed an open mind for, but I was willing, and a little half way through the book I found a key section that helped me move forward.

It was about forgiveness. She wrote about the benefits of forgiveness and releasing the bindings attached to you with old wounds or negative connections. She explained that to forgive is not the same as "to lose" or to say "I was wrong, you were right". It is not "letting someone or something off the hook" for a wrongdoing - It is the process of freeing your spirit from the attached negative bindings.

This made sense to me and for the first time in our son's life, I felt that I could forgive autism. Autism was still a huge presence in our home. I needed to cut the negative vibes of autism and all the fear, pain, crap and uncertainty it had brought into our lives. The moments and future dreams autism had robbed from our family, but mostly Jonathan. I needed to forgive autism so it wouldn't hurt or control me or mine any more and when I did, I never looked back.

I started to learn techniques on how to "cut negative energy cords" and learn to forgive without feeling as if I were "giving in or failing". I worked on forgiving autism, the school, judgmental people, the doctors, the vaccinations…and more. I started to heal.

I started meditating (after many lifetime attempts) and for the first time, I learned to calm my mind and body. I found out that Tami Duncan started to broadcast a free, weekly meditation segment for the Autism Community focusing on topics I could relate to. Using techniques from Tami, I was meditating every day and I would have visions of Archangel Raphael, whose name means, "God heals", and his color of brilliant green always greeting my sessions.

I was finding the missing pieces of MY puzzle. I started to read, research and learn how to "let go" and release my guilt about autism and letting Jonathan get too many vaccinations too soon and the assault of antibiotics that wiped out the beneficial flora in his gut. My guilt about not knowing about GMO soy baby formula being so toxic as his main food source the first year of his developmental stages, about GMO corn and all the other environmental toxins he endured in his young life.

After a few weeks of daily meditations, I would have clear visions of my fellow Autism Moms on mats, meditating, doing yoga and "unloading their emotions" in a safe environment of no judgments with other Moms who understood their journeys. It was so clear and the message so strong, that I put together two Parent-to-Parent workshops called:

## *Autism Mom's PMS Workshop (Positive Mind Set)*

The workshops were well received and after the very first one, I knew I was going down my divine path: I needed to help Heal the Autism Moms, and in turn, the children will heal along by their sides.

I had visions of Jonathan teaching other ASD children how to communicate with their parents using his video lingo he had taught me, so I created my first video workshop called "Talking in Videos...an Autism Language"[9]. I constructed a step-by-step method to identify, decode, and translate video language into everyday lingo to help build communication with ASD children.

MY Puzzle of life, started to come together. When I began this journey, I felt alone. I had a "Good Luck" kiss-off from our pediatrician and was sent on my way. That was over 12 years ago. I never wanted another parent to feel as alone as I did that day and I wanted there to be more help for us all.

Today, I still see younger parents and their children being introduced to the world of autism and it breaks my heart to know the road they will be traveling; but it is because of courageous parents and children who refuse to give up, that we have a community that will not be silent.

We are not accepting "good luck" answers and "institution" futures for our children. We are making changes in government, environment, our food supply, and education. These children whose

---

[9] "Talking in Videos...an Autism Language" can be found at www.MyAutismHatRack.com

voices may have limited-verbal capabilities, are shouting to the World the need for mankind to love one another, understand differences and heal the Earth.

I have made peace with God & autism. I do not like the pain, fear and physical ailments thwarted on our children in the guise of autism, but autism is a man-made, multilevel inflicted disease and not brought on by God.

The principal lesson learned, on this journey into the autism world, is the more I celebrate the JOYS of who Jonathan IS and not spotlight "who he ISN'T", healing began.

Then, in the universal "Life Flip", Jonathan became the one healing his armor clad, Warrior Mama everyday.

CHAPTER 14

## MY AUTISM OUTLOOK

*"If you change the way you look at things,
the things you look at change."*
- WAYNE DYER

Autism has given me an entirely new outlook on life and our living. I have always been a very positive person, always looking for the bright side to a situation. The funny thing was, I thought I was very productive too…until autism and the journey it has taken me on.

I can honestly say, that without the awareness of autism and the health problems our son has gone through, I never would have delved into environmental issues with as much passion. I never would have questioned the medical field and our pediatrician on their advice and schedules of vaccinations, if I hadn't seen the damage it did to Jonathan. I never would have looked at ingredients on food items and package goods like I do. I NEVER would have cared what my child's poop looked like, much less try and capture it for fecal samples of biological tests.

Without autism, I never would have known what an IEP was. Special Education was foreign to me, but I advocated legally for our son's FAPE/Homebound education and testified in front of the Texas State Senate Committee in favor of Autism Education Bills. I never would have done any of these things as passionately as I do them now, for myself…but for our child- I will knock down barriers all day long.

At the beginning of this journey, I felt like a victim, weak, pissed-off and hopeless. I hated autism and everything that came with it. Gut issues, migraines, verbal language challenges, sleepless nights, erratic behaviors, scream-fests, hitting, biting…all of it- but I love our child.

Autism is scary. It is a 6-letter word that neatly labels a plethora of neurological, biomedical, emotional, and environmental ailments, upon a generation of children. Autism is an epidemic disease that has attacked newborns, toddlers, families, communities, and generations. It does not discriminate by race, sex, or demographics.

At last count, the US CDC's studies have announced 1 in 50 children have autism; this study is based on children who are 8-10 years old in 2010. Being that it is 2013, I personally believe that the epidemic of autism reaches 1 in 25 children easy. You have differing degrees of the spectrum, but even the CDC publishes[10] that 1 in 6 children in the US have a learning disability, speech impairment, ADHD, ADD, PDD-NOS, Aspergers or Autism. This means, that if you know more than 50 people in your life circle, then you know someone with autism or someone whose child has autism. This is scary as shit.

But, the love of a Mother, Father, brother or sister is what will make you look past the scary part of autism and see your beautiful child. The love for your child is what will make you fight for a better life, answers, treatments, and solutions. Jonathan has gone from "severe, non-verbal autism diagnosis" to "moderate autism" with high language skills. He has done this through alternative medical approaches, supplements, organic diet, environmental detoxification and perseverance to communicate.

---

[10] Source: CDC online http://www.cdc.gov/ncbddd/autism/data.html

Jonathan can speak now and he tells me "he is not Autism" and that "Autism is broken". He is right. Autism is a man made, environmental assault on our child…BUT OUR CHILD IS NOT AUTISM. Our child is funny, happy, creative, amazing and loving to all that he meets. He has taught me so much in his short lifetime to change generations to come.

Years ago, a lady said to me, trying to be comforting, "Maureen, you are so strong and remember, God only gives you what you can handle".

I thought that was bullshit. God would never want anyone to "handle" autism and the harm it does to our babies and families. God doesn't give us the toxins attacking our children. God blesses us with a beautiful soul wrapped in the gift of a child, for us to take care of and nurture. It is up to us to make the right decisions for our children's care and clean up our environment so we can all live healthier lives.

**Autism is NOT a gift.** To me, that is like saying Cancer is a gift. MS is a gift. Diabetes is a gift. I relate Autism to a disease harming my child and thousands more; Autism is NOT a gift.

**The GIFT** is Jonathan.

**The GIFT** is your child and every milestone they achieve.

**The GIFTS** are the people I have met, learned from, cried with and loved on this "Life Flip".

**The GIFTS** are the truths of information I have learned about our food, vaccines, government, special education, pharmaceutical companies and medical community.

**The GIFTS** are the Autism Parent's spirit and love for their child and the lengths they will go to make a better life for their loved ones.

**The GIFTS** are the changes I have seen in the world as people accept these beautiful children instead of shunning them as damaged.

Open your mind and your heart and see these beautiful children for who they are:
> loving, trusting, kind, funny, creative, amazing, brilliant and literal thinkers. They are a **GIFT** to be unraveled, appreciated, loved and treasured.

*Jonathan is my gift and I am still unwrapping him.*

*Hope, Dream, Believe...Today!*

# PART II

*My "Hats"*

The following "Hats" have been accumulating for years and with every "Hat", there is a purpose to make life better, ignite hope and heal yourself and your loved ones. As a caretaker of an "extra needs" child, you will wear many different "Hats" but ONLY YOU can take the initiative and make a difference in your life and your child's.

Put your "Hats" on TODAY!

Blessings & Stay Strong,

*Maureen*


*"Finish every day and be done with it. You have done what you could. Some blunders and absurdities no doubt have crept in; forget them as soon as you can. Tomorrow is a new day; begin it well and serenely and with too high a spirit to be cumbered with your old nonsense. This day is all that is good and fair. It is too dear, with its hopes and invitations,*
*to waste a moment on yesterdays."*
- RALPH WALDO EMERSON


**More "Hats" can be found on www.MyAutismHatRack.com**

## CHAPTER 15

## THE "MAMA HAT"...A LETTER TO JONATHAN

The "Mama Hat" is a Hat worn with so many emotions and adventures associated with it. Joy, excitement, pride, wonderment, fear, anxiety, progress, success, failures - relating to all your children. I always want to stress that before taking on the challenges of autism, you must see your beautiful child. Their love, humor, happiness, giggles, determination and their beautiful souls.

I want to share a letter I have written to Jonathan for him to read and understand when he is ready. Now take all your "Hats" off for a moment and don't think of the "whys" & "hows" of autism causes and treatments.

When things get a little stressful, read this letter I have written to our son and gain a little more strength to put your "Mama Hat" on! Love to ALL the Amazing Mamas and their beautiful children~

*Dearest Jonathan,*

*You came to me as a gift from God with happiness in your heart. You trusted me to take care of you and love you every day, to protect you from things that may harm you and teach you how to maneuver your way through this world. The moment I felt you kick in my belly, I was thrilled that you had chosen me and our family to be a part of your beautiful soul's journey.*

*I know we have had hiccups along the road of our adventures, but I've never let go of your hand or your heart. I will be there for you when you're sad and happy. I will be there for you when you are confused and clear minded. I will be there for you if you fail and when you succeed. I will be there for you always, for the Universe has brought you to me and me to you.*

*We have a mission to heal and be blissful. We have wishes to fulfill and present moments to enjoy. You have taught me so many lessons in this lifetime, that sometimes our roles have been reversed as "teacher and student" but every day with you is a gift that I treasure with appreciation and gratitude. I am honored to be your Mama.*

*Love smoochies to you, Jonathan. Catch them all, in my heart, from the start...never to part.*
    *I love you,*
*Mama*

CHAPTER 16

## THE "PMS HAT"
### ...CHANGING THE ACRONYM & MIND SET!

We can all basically agree that Autism can be difficult, scary, negative, frustrating and in Jonathan's own words, "Autism is broken"...**BUT, Your Child is NOT Autism**. Your Child is amazing, beautiful, unique, loving, funny, and a survivor. There are differences of opinion on how children developed autism. In our journey, Jonathan is a vaccine-injured baby that destroyed his immune system and environmental toxins attacked- I have no doubt. I was there.

Today is your day to put on your "PMS Hat". PMS = Positive Mind Set (had you thinking there for a minute :0). If you do not have this Hat on your Autism HatRack, you will find it hard to be happy.

You will be doing a disservice to your child. You may not be giving him/her the most beautiful life they are capable of having. I know this first hand. I lived in negativity and misery for years. That was all it took for me to realize I was doing nothing for my family except weighing down the atmosphere with my crappy moods and anger.

I was furious at Jonathan's doctors/vaccines for the toxin poisoning, jealous of friend's kids the same age for "being normal", irritated with family members for being evasive and absent (*not their fault; I had no idea what I needed from them*), the universe for the injustice of it all....Well, you know where it got me? Alone, depressed and miserable. It was the BIGGEST waste of time, and when you are dealing with Autism- time is precious.

A child with Autism feeds off emotions, energy and vibes. They are extremely sensitive to their surroundings, even if you don't think they are aware of anything. They absorb all of it and that is why situations can be so overwhelming for them at times. So how do you think your child will be when their surroundings are emitting negative vibes? Well, get ready because he/she will give negative right back. And in our case, since Jonathan used sounds and squeals instead of words, the negative came back with a vengeance in the form of a "scream-fest".

The "PMS Hat" is a blindly optimistic Mind Set. You need to think POSITIVE! It is not easy. You have to make an effort to sift through the bad junk and highlight the positive treasures:

- **Negative**: your child just made poop-art on the bathroom wall next to the toilet.
- **Positive**: You have been potty training him/her for 6 months and he/she just demonstrated a "landing in the toilet" and eye &

hand coordination! Whoo Hoo! Grab the organic house cleaner of your choice, paper towels and celebrate!
- **Negative:** Your child broke into the pantry and ate an entire box of organic cookies.
- **Positive:** At least he went for the organic ones instead of the Oreos you had stashed behind the gluten-free flour.
- **Negative (actually more irritating than negative)**: You child runs, jumps, hops, spins - it would drive any parent crazy. Put on your "PMS Hat" and take it to the
- **Positive**:
   1) If they run - race your child up the stairs or across the yard. Make it interactive and purposeful.
   2) If they flap - flap your arms with your child when they get excited. They feel a connection and will think it is fun and not weird.
   3) If they hop, hop with your child and start counting hops as you do it. It instills counting and rhythmic methods and a connection between you and him/her.
- **Negative:** A teacher once said, "Jonathan really isn't doing well with following his lines and shapes. so he had to stay at the table until he did it right." She said it as a negative punishment for his messy tactics.
- **Positive:** I was disappointed with the teacher's negative attitude, not Jonathan. I was excited he stayed at the table and used a pencil displaying fine motor skills.

Take the words/phrases: "No", "That is wrong", "Quit doing that", "Stop that" - all negative responses out of your vocabulary. Your child is learning to build their self- esteem, confidence and self-awareness. Use phrases like "Good job", "You are doing great", "That's wonderful, can you do it another way?"

**The "PMS Hat" is a must have Hat on your Autism HatRack. Positive thinking, attitude and vibes will make things move forward just like a "+" sign adds things up.**

**The only thing a negative point of view will do, is subtract your progress, love and patience on this journey.**

There is nothing *Positive* about being *Negative*.

CHAPTER 17

# THE "IMMUNOLOGIST HAT"
## ...THE BIOMEDICAL TESTS

I strongly suggest you test your child for allergies. This needs to be your child's VERY FIRST TEST! Before NutraEval, ONE test, Poop Tests, Heavy Metals Toxin Tests, etc...

Why? Because if your child starts to get treated for nutritional deficiencies or a new protocol, he/she will be running in circles if he/she is allergic to any of supplements or foods they are consuming – TEST YOUR CHILD'S ALLERGIES FIRST!

You can order allergy blood test through your Pediatrician, Immunologist, Family Practitioner, GI, DAN Doctor (Defeat Autism Now) or MAP Doctor (Medical Academy of Pediatric Special Needs).

We found out that Jonathan was allergic to Soy, Dairy, Eggs (he never should have gotten any vaccines due to an egg allergy - Doctors know this fact but never bother to test infants for egg allergies before immunizations), Gluten, Wheat grains (yes, different from gluten), Corn, Rice, Yeast, Sugar, Beef, Pork, Shrimp, Fish, Walnuts, Carrots, Watermelon, Oats, Pinto Beans, Oranges, Bananas, Soap, Grass, Dust, Pollen.... the list went on and on. We had gone from a little boy with Autism to the "Boy in the Bubble" Travolta movie.

Some signs of food allergies can be:

•Red cheeks- this is a flush that appears and stays on your child

when they have touched or eaten a food they are allergic too.
- •Red Ears & Tips of Ears - this was a wild indicator for an allergy to Corn (including corn/vegetable oil). When Jonathan would eat corn tortilla chips- his ears would flare up like they were on fire and he would get angry or impatient within minutes. Corn tortilla + corn oil = mad little boy!
- •Clear runny nose - this happened with peanut butter, saltines crackers, outside pollen, apple juice, orange juice (even organic) or any food that had a powdery coating-like smarties candies or flavored chips.

Your "Immunologist Hat" will help give you answers to help build your child's immune system.

**Biomedical Tests** - There are so many biomedical tests you need to do on your child to get a starting point and reference of their deficiencies, methylation cycle and bio make up. Below is a "to do" test list in a specific order to help understand what your child will need bio medically and how they will absorb, detox, and benefit from certain supplements, pharmaceuticals and therapies.
*(Please check with your healthcare practitioner when ordering any biomedical tests.)*

**- IgG Food Antibody Assessment & IgE Food and Environmental/Inhalant Allergy Assessment blood Tests** – We cycled for years giving our son supplements based off of his deficiencies in basic Amino Acids, Proteins, and Glutathione tests, but we found he was allergic to some of the supplements, so sometimes he would have a negative reaction. These tests will show the sensitivities in your child's system so you can apply the supplements that your child will absorb and benefit from.

**- EDS - Electrodermal Screening Testing** is a non-invasive data acquisition process, which measures electrical currents in the body much like an EKG machine measures the electrical activity of the heart. The computerized EDS device measures the electron flow throughout the body allowing the technician to conduct an "interview" with the body's organs and tissues. These readings are taken from pathways near the surface of the skin known as meridians, where the electromagnetic energy generated in the internal organs circulates throughout the body.

**- NutrEval Test – by Genova Diagnostics** - This is the test that will give you answers as to the nutritional markers of your child. It includes levels and absorption of Amino Acids, Antioxidants, Vitamins, Minerals, Essential Fatty Acids Krebs Cycle, Toxin Markers, Cellular Energy and Mitochondrial Metabolites, etc…

**- Genetic BioMarker tests** –Genetics do play a part in your child's healing. The latest studies on Epigenetic information are fascinating and prove genetics can change in a generation due to our environmental toxins.

You will want to get genetic markers on your child and the "blueprint" of your child's Methylation Cycle. This cycle will show pathways and blockages in your child's ability to detoxify heavy radicals.

You can order this test directly from these two companies. The prices vary, but the genetic results are sent back to you with a method of deciphering the genetic synapses:

www.23andMe.com

www.DrAmyYasko.com


To find doctors near you please check these links from:

**GENERATION RESCUE-**
http://www.generationrescue.org/resources/find-a-physician/

**TACA-TALK ABOUT CURING AUTISM:**
http://www.tacanow.org/blog/treating-autism-maps-doctors-dan-doctors/

Nutrient Power by Dr. William Walsh is a great book to read and learn about Epigenetics, biochemistry and the brain.

**Quicksilver Scientific** - Dr. Chris Shade explains how mercury and heavy metal toxins affect the brain and gut in his video blogs on www.vimeo.com - search: Quicksilver Scientific.
www.QuicksilverScientific.com

**Brainworx** – Dr. Homero Cavazos interprets and explains nutritional, biological tests to parents in a way they can understand. He is a located in the Plano, Texas area. www.Brainworx.com

CHAPTER 18

## THE "WHAT DIET NOW? HAT"

Through the years, more and more "natural" foods are being replaced by fast food restaurants on every corner, frozen TV dinners, packaged cookies, jarred sauces - all loaded with preservatives. Before Autism, I didn't think much of it. I mean who didn't love a Twinkie every now and then? Grabbing lunch or dinner at a drive through with Kid Meals on the menu, was easy and with the schedules we kept, it was beginning to be the norm.

I had to start breaking down diet and nutrition when Jonathan was only a few months old after he got whooping cough and had a round of antibiotics. He had a terrible case of thrush and our Pediatrician told me to stop breast-feeding him because I was doing him more harm than good. So, I started baby formula and he was constantly throwing it up and only keeping a few ounces down. Our Pediatrician then said, he must have a lactose intolerance, feed him soy formula, so I did.

*Can you imagine how horrified I was when I found out after doing Jonathan's allergy tests, that he was allergic to soy baby formula? All those months of neurodevelopment stages and he was allergic to his main nutritional supplement. (Get the allergy tests done!)*

*Then in 2012, I saw a documentary on GMO (Genetically Modified Organisms) foods called* Genetic Roulette the Movie *(www.GeneticRouletteMovie.com) and I found out the brand of soy baby formula I had given to Jonathan from 3 months to 18 months (crucial brain developmental stages), was made with 86% GMO neurotoxin-chemical soy. Translation: Jonathan was getting 86% soy made with the same chemicals found in Round Up weed killer! It never said that crap in the label that I could understand! Between vaccines, GMO soy baby formula and allergies, Jonathan didn't have a chance for a normal developmental and detoxification system (MAJOR hindsight- so learn from our journey).*

Remember, Jonathan was born perfect and healthy according to his Pediatrician and medical records in August 2000. So how could a baby be so allergic to almost everything, even things he had never eaten? He now had a compromised immune system, so I took him off soy formula & soymilk and I got eye contact! Not very long time frames, but long enough to see those beautiful blue-green eyes connect to mine for a few seconds.

So I went into full NEW diet mode and according to his skin tests, he was allergic to basically everything. FIRST MISTAKE - I did a list of everything he was allergic to and started looking. **DO NOT DO THIS!** Instead, make a list of the foods your child is **NOT allergic** to and then make a list of 5 to 10 items of food he/she **CAN EAT** - this is so much easier and less over whelming.

Even though you have 20/20 vision, buy a magnifying glass you can carry in your purse or bag to be able to read the ingredients on the labels. The typeface can get tiny and you will read words with 5 or more syllables you can't pronounce.

The first time you go into a store after deciding to RE-DO your child's nutrition, give yourself a 2 hour window and go by yourself. Take a smart phone to take pictures of items and make a visual grocery list.

Many mainstream grocery stores carry Gluten-Free packaged

products now, which can be helpful. I personally don't buy many packaged goods at all. The preservatives are so bad for Jonathan; I found it much easier to stick to organic/non-gmo fresh foods, fruits, and vegetables.

You want to cycle the foods he/she can have. Try not to make every meal chicken or whatever protein they can eat. If you are not careful, it has been proven that your child can create an allergy to a food if they are saturated with it.

Take out any foods that have these items in the label because they are used as a chemical preservative:

- High Fructose Corn syrup
- Any foods containing Corn or Soy as it has a 90% chance of being Genetically Modified Organisms (GMO) and full of chemical toxins. Also a great resource about GMO Foods is the Non GMO Project www.nongmoproject.org
- Soy Lecithin
- Sugar Free Products – very deceptive because most are made with Sugar Alcohol (made from corn). You have a better chance going with a food made from organic cane sugar or honey for your child to process in their digestive system.

Through the years I have had to itemize Jonathan's diet, we have tried the: Gluten/Casein free diet, SCD diet, Low Oxalate Diet, GMO Free, sugar free diet, yeast free diet, soy free, the "pull my hair out because I'm going crazy" diet...the most important things I concluded from all these diets are:

Stick with fresh, organic, NON-GMO foods: fruits, veggies, chicken, turkey, or non-tainted fresh fish (not tuna).

- Try NOT to feed your child packaged goods – there are so many chemicals listed in the ingredients that your child might be sensitive too, just pass on it until you can boost your child's digestive system to break down the allergen foods.
- At restaurants- order meat, veggies or fruit- plain. If you go for chicken nuggets-ask if the flour is gluten-free and you don't want anything fried in vegetable oil or soy oil. Grape-seed and coconut oil are easier for little tummies to breakdown.
- Always carry a digestive enzyme to give your child at mealtime or between meals. Jonathan is sensitive to Protease; it is in all the digestive enzymes, (which explained why some worked and some didn't). So, he gets a peppermint & fennel Young Living Essential Oil capsule for his meals and it helps his digestive system.

Please watch the documentary Genetic Roulette to be informed before you eat another bite! **Www.GeneticRouletteMovie.com.**

**Some great Information References are:**
Special Diets for Special Kids by Lisa Lewis, Ph.D.
Children with Starving Brains by Jacquelyn McCandles, M.D.
Incredible Edible Gluten-Free Food for Kids by Sheri L. Sanderson
The Allergy Self-Help Cookbook by Marjorie Hurt Jones, RN
Lox Oxidate  http://www.nutrition-healing.com/lowoxalate.html

*As I stated at the beginning of this book, I am not a medical healthcare professional, nor a nutritionist. Every section of advice is from experience, trial and error. Please make your own decisions on what diets you choose and foods you want your family to consume, but let your Mama Gut lead the way.*

CHAPTER 19

## THE "ESSENTIAL OILS AND AUTISM HAT"

I remember looking at our son, Jonathan's tests results taken at 2 ½ years old, and seeing his yeast was off the charts. Not only did he have yeast in his internal system, but he also had rashes all over his body. We had implemented a steroid cream, diflucan and nystatin through our doctor, but the yeast was a beast we could not eliminate.

I started to look up Candida on the internet and I found that tea tree essential oil was a natural antifungal, so I drove to the health food store and purchased an over-the-counter tea tree essential oil.

That night, I mixed up and applied the tea tree oil with a grape seed, carrier oil concoction, all over Jonathan's body and by the next morning, his rashes were gone!

That was it for me. I was sold on essential oils (EOs). I delved into studying about essential oils and asked a local naturopath about them. She informed me that there were different kinds of EOs and I needed to invest in therapeutic, pure grade EOs because some EOs were made with additional chemicals.

I acted upon her recommendation and researched a few popular brands. Based off of third party testing and results, I started using Young Living Essential Oils (YLEOs) because I was concentrating on getting harmful chemicals out of our family, not back in. Through the years, we have used YLEOs to treat everything in our home from Autism, ADHD, OCD, allergies, gout, rashes, anxiety, fevers, flu, acne, strep, and more, **replacing all over the counter/prescription medicines.**

In March 2010, we took Jonathan to our GI for an endoscope. Due to his extreme allergies, stress, and other issues, the GI scoped him and found his esophagus completely swollen and inflamed. She did a biopsy and he was diagnosed with Eosinophilic Esophagitis (EE), chronic gastritis, and acid reflux. His treatment was an immediate liquid diet (you can only imagine how fun that was with a sensory issue kiddo) and an allergist wanted to treat him with antigen shots to build his immune system. The problem with that was, Jonathan was so allergic and internally inflamed, any antigen treatment could result in anaphylaxis shock - So, that was not an option.

I turned to my YLEOs because I knew Jonathan responded well to them and the brand I use, Young Living, could be ingested and I needed to treat him from the inside - out. (Please note that most over-the-counter EOs CANNOT be taken internally, read the labels prior to application).

Autism mirrors a plethora of physical, emotional and cognitive symptoms and now with Jonathan's EE diagnosis, I needed to target symptoms that eventually would help heal his "Autism issues". Starting with Jonathan's serve inflammation and allergies, I used YLEO Lavender and Eucalyptus Globulus. I applied these oils topically, aromatically and in a capsule. I found that Lavender (a natural antihistamine) actually helped calm Jonathan down because it addressed his allergies, which were triggering his anxiety to escalate. Eucalyptus Globulus helps with respiratory and sinus issues as an antibacterial, antiviral, and antifungal and would help reduce his EE inflammation. I would alternate with Lemon, to help kill any viruses or chemicals he was exposed to.

Allergies were just the first target of treatment in this stage of healing for Jonathan. His emotional and cognitive processing was in regression mode. YL Frankincense is **extremely high in sesquiterpenes** and can cross the blood-brain barrier to the limbic part of the brain. This meant that he could take this EO and it would help "Zen" his mind. Frankincense helped with his Post Traumatic Stress Disorder and anxiety. This was huge for us because I did not give our son any SSRIs as prescribed by his psychiatrist; we needed to heal him with natural ingredients.

Next up were Jonathan's gut issues with his chronic gastritis, acid reflux and digestion. I would put YLEO Peppermint in capsules with Fennel to aid in Jonathan's digestion and help breakdown food proteins he had such a hard time absorbing. Then I would alternate with YL DiGize that blends 8 YLEOs to target digestion, heartburn, gas, bloating, Candida and kills parasite infestation. This helped build his immune system in his gut. Now that Jonathan is older, he takes YL Detoxzyme capsules that are enzymes with YLEOs that he absorbs very well and also help eliminate any heavy metals he may ingest in food or water.

I continued applying YLEO blends to him: Peace and Calming & RutaVala Roll on his spine, bottom feet and toes, lymph nodes at the neck and armpits, before bedtime to help him sleep. Valor in the mornings to help align his spinal fluid and desensitize his nervous system, Brain Power before his studies at the base of his brain stem with gentle strokes upwards to activate the nerve endings and Thieves to help build his immune system against viruses and bacteria.

There are hundreds of Young Living Essential Oils you can use to help your child with symptoms that affect cognitive, physical and emotional issues and as most of us know, each child will absorb and react to things differently depending on their biochemistry.

Our entire family benefits from using YLEOs (even the four legged ones) topically, internally and aromatically. When Gregory would come home from High School complaining of a sore throat and chills, I would start him on an YLEO Lemon, Thieves, Eucalyptus Globulus and RC remedy and in 2-3 days he was back to normal and had missed the Strep & Mono going around school. Then I would put the whole family on the remedy to make sure our immune systems were strong.

If you are looking for a natural approach to healing many ailments in your family, try Essential Oils. Please note that my testimonials are based on Young Living Essential Oils. YLEOs are not sold over the counter but you can purchase through a Distributor, Naturopath or online. Make sure you purchase YLEOs with someone you know who can help guide you with recipes, info and support. It is key that you learn how to use EOs, no matter what brand you choose. My experience with EOs has been life changing and fundamental to our family's health.

*The YLEO recipes mentioned above can be found in the Essential Oils Pocket Reference guide by Gary Young, Young Living; Published by Life Science Publishing. The information above is not intended to diagnosis, as treatment or prescription for any disease, nor is it an alternative to regular medical attention. If medical attention is needed, please contact a health professional.*

Chapter 20

## The "Wonder Mama Headband"

### Cuffs, Lasso, Boots, Airplane – It Takes the Whole Outfit!

*Artwork by Danielle Brice Bordelon*

Technically, Wonder Woman wears a metal headband/crown on her head instead of a hat, but since I find myself transforming into Wonder Mama to play an occasional Super Hero for all 3 of our kids...it is a definite "Hat" on My Autism Hat Rack.

Wonder Mama uses her pair of indestructible bracelet cuffs, an invisible airplane, a Lasso of Truth, which forces those bound by it to tell the truth, Rockin' Red Boots, and a Golden Headband which serves as a protective angel halo.

**Things you will need for your Wonder Mama outfit in the world of Autism:**

**1) Indestructible Bracelet Cuffs**- yes these do come in handy and all you guys out there, get your minds out of the gutter. These cuffs are made of indestructible metal and can deflect any bullet thrown at your child: Not a "bullet' will pierce your child as you will learn to wave your hands like a crazy woman deflecting glares, ignorant words, and judgmental advice.

**2) The Invisible Airplane-** this comes in handy both on the ground and in the air:

When you are on an airplane and your child's ears can't pop, their head hurts, they need to jump or hop, he/she doesn't understand why they can't keep hitting the seat in front of them with the "meal-tray toy" offered to them, because it is so cool how the tray can go up & down. You will transport yourselves into your Invisible Airplane where you will apply brushing strokes, deep pressure hand squeezes, and comfort your child from pain and anxiety. You will become invisible to the 250 judgmental glares that could not even begin to understand your plight.

You will use this plane when you are in a grocery store and your child sees a box of cookies that has been removed from their diet but they remember those yummy cookies because your child has a photographic memory...and a scream that could break glass comes from your grocery cart. You will want this plane to transport you and your child, as you casually, as if nothing is askew, make your way to the check out counter and buy those dang groceries you need to make dinner. Your WM Invisible Airplane will protect you until you are out the automatic doors.

**3) The Golden Lasso of Truth** - This is a very powerful tool- so only use it when you want to know the Truth!

We used this lasso to get the truth out of Jonathan's Special Education Teacher, aides and school Principal. With the lies being told, negligence being covered up, violations of his education, I used the Golden Lasso and the truth revealed the illegal restraint, confinement and harm done to Jonathan. No matter how terrible the truth was, I needed to know it so I could help heal Jonathan from anxieties and fears.

**4) The Rockin' Red Boots** - You will wear these boots while humming the song by Nancy Sinatra "These Boots are made for walking".

You will wear these boots for your school ARD Meetings to stomp out inappropriate goals and BIP tactics for your child's IEP.

You will wear these boots at Autism Seminars where you will strut from one seminar to 10 other seminars soaking in the information from therapists, scientists and parents, all with their "piece of the puzzle" information and expertise.

You will wear these boots as you testify in front of State Senate & House of Representatives Committees on behalf of Autism Education Bills.

You will wear these boots the first day you leave your child at a daycare/PPCD/preschool, because you will need their power to help you walk away as you let go of your angel's hand and watch them smile and run into the room of children and not look back.

You will wear these Boots while you stomp over the hurdles of Autism through the years!

**5) The Red, White and Blue Corset Outfit**- You will wear this to help keep your girlie figure in check as you are nurturing your family's health and days at the gym are a memory.

AND FINALLY....

**The Golden Headband** - This is the headband you will wear as your Earth Angel protective halo. You will be reminded that God is only a thought or prayer away, Mother Mary is always ready to give you guidance and support and Your Angel Posse is waiting in the wings to help, just ask -WEAR IT PROUD!

CHAPTER 21

## MY "HOPE, DREAM, BELIEVE HAT"

When Jonathan was about 8 years old, another Mom raising a child with autism, said to me, "What are you doing with Jonathan? He is doing so well. You make it all look so easy!"

My immediate reaction was laughter. I thought, "Holy crap, if I make this autism adventure look easy, then I wanted my golden Oscar". Nothing has been easy. From the gut wrenching cries at 3 months old, whooping-cough (after DTaP) with 106 degree fevers, sleepless nights and erratic outbursts, lack and then loss of language, eye contact, lack of interaction, poop smeared walls, raising 2 neuro-typical kids to love their little brother with his "hiccups"...to the years of therapies, diets, biomedical treatments, insurance battles for coverage, advocating for appropriate special education, the "Harvard" tuition we have spent for his ABA and other approaches..."EASY" is not a word I have ever associated with autism! But this Warrior Mom saw my Jonathan as an "easy" little boy.

I looked across the room where Jonathan was playing with his blue letters, spelling out video titles and thought- Jonathan wasn't having a "scream-fest" (took 7 years to crack that code), his tics/OCD stems were minimal, he was requesting things clearly with 5 or more words, he was interacting and engaging with others and his compliance was at an all time high.

I looked at this Mom and her eyes started to tear up and she said, "I hope my son will say what he wants someday, or just say, "I love you Mommy!"

Whack! Talk about knife to the heart! I SO remember wanting that same wish years ago! She instantly took me back to when Jonathan was 4 years old and I was buckling him into his car seat. It was Mother's Day and I got an amazing gift: Jonathan looked me in the eyes and said, "I love you Mama". It was the first time he had ever said, "I love you" unprompted. Time froze for a brief moment- "I love you Mama!" Still, a cherished moment, in my lifetime, from our limited verbal child.

All I could do was hug her and let her know that I knew exactly how she felt. Autism is not easy. It is not for the weak of heart, faith or spirit. autism chews you up and spits you out. BUT- autism is NOT YOUR CHILD! Your beautiful child is there and you CAN NOT lose sight of that. You have to look past the tantrums, screams, anxiety, poop-art AND see the love, humor, hope, brilliant mind suppressed by the fog of autism. You have to be POSITIVE because your child feels that energy and will respond to it.

I have **HOPE** for her son that he will someday tell his mother what he wants and the cherished words every mother wants to hear; "I love you Mama".

I **DREAM** that all of our children challenged with autism will find their voices one way or another in their lifetime and express their inner most amazing thoughts!

I **BELIEVE** in our children and their beautiful souls - they want their voices heard. You, the parent and/or caregiver, will be the facilitator to make these things come true.

You must stay strong along this journey of *The Life Flip* because your child will need a safe, loving, beautiful place to land and grow. Your child will need YOU! Now put your "Hope Hat" on and go…

## Start Your Own Autism HatRack Today!

## THERAPIES ON "MY AUTISM HAT RACK"

Living within the world of Autism, I have added multiple therapies on My Autism Hat Rack. With each therapy, I had to become a Parent Professional in the management, application and development of the therapies. Why? Because Jonathan was pre-verbal and I had to monitor the results of each therapy to record progress, regression and/or success.

These therapies have each played a part in our healing journey. As unique as a fingerprint, so are our children. Because biology, diet and environment all attribute to the healing of your child's autism symptoms, some things may help you and some may not. Get your Autism Hat Rack ready to hang a lot of different hats, but always go with your gut on what works for your child.

Listed below are some of the therapies/protocols we have implemented in the last 12+ years that made significant impact on Jonathan's healing and milestones:

- **NAET –Nambudripad's Allergy Elimination Techniques**:
  Nambudripad's Allergy Elimination Techniques, also known as NAET®, are a non-invasive, drug free, natural solution to alleviate allergies of all types and intensities using a blend of selective energy balancing, testing and treatment procedures from acupuncture/acupressure, chiropractic, nutritional, and kinesiological disciplines of medicine.
  Find your local therapist in North America:
  http://www.naet.com/subscribers/drnamerica.html

- **Occupational Therapy – with Sensory Integration Approach**

    OT is extremely important to build your child's physical awareness, build confidence, self-esteem and help desensitize a hypo/hyper sensory system. We have used many therapists through the years and you need to find a great one that understands your child's sensory needs.

    Betsy Williams at TOP in Frisco, Texas is a crucial angel on Jonathan's Healing Team.

    http://www.toppediatrictherapy.com/

- **Applied Behavior Analysis Therapy (ABA)** – ABA is one of the few researched based therapies for Autism behavior. We did 2 years of ABA therapy combining an in-home program and a Center for ABA. I total support the ABA philosophy; however, I found out quickly that the "applied" part of ABA, is crucial based on your therapists.

    We started an in-home ABA program in 2004 as we waited for openings to be available at ABA centers in our area. 6 months into our in-home ABA program, a spot opened up at Behavioral Innovations and we enrolled Jonathan right away. The Center was run by BCBAs and had trained therapists ready to do their jobs and we found taking Jonathan to a center was a beneficial routine. We drove 3 hours a day to get Jonathan to and from the center, but the year he was there, was a good experience.

    I personally recommend ABA methods intermingled with social skills, RDI and positive reinforcement will generate a successful ABA therapy investment.

    http://behavioral-innovations.com/

- **Speech Therapy – Applied using Sensory Approach.** When you have a pre-verbal child, the first thing you want to do is speech, but if your child can not sit at a table, follow verbal directions or has cognitive processing issues, you are frustrating your child and wasting your money. Attend to the therapies above first and then find a speech therapist educated in autism that has a POSITIVE demeanor and patience. Remember you do not want to work on annunciating words and sounds right away, you are working on your child's cognitive processing of words and their meanings. Articulation will come later.
- **Relationship Development Intervention (RDI)**
  RDI is a behavioral intervention for autism developed by Dr. Steven Gutstein. The initial goal is to build a guided participation relationship between parents and child, with the child as a "cognitive apprentice." Once this relationship is in place, the family advances through a series of developmental goals for their child. According to Dr. Gutstein, this process improves "neural connectivity," or brain function. RDI is a fundamental therapy for your child and family. Look for a local RDI therapist or center in your area.
- **EDS** - Electrodermal Screening (EDS) – This is a blueprint of your child's internal system. As mentioned in Chapter 17, EDS is a non-invasive data acquisition process which measures electrical currents in the body much like an EKG machine measures the electrical activity of the heart. The computerized EDS device measures the electron flow throughout the body allowing the technician to conduct an "interview" with the body's organs and tissues. These readings are taken from

pathways near the surface of the skin known as meridians, where the electromagnetic energy generated in the internal organs circulates throughout the body. The treatments are homeopathic remedies, supplements and diet.

Danette Goodyear as been our EDS practitioner for many years and is an earth angel on Jonathan's Healing Team. www.NorthTexasDynamicHealth.com

- **HBOT**– Hyperbaric Oxygen Therapy was something we did when Jonathan was 5 years old. We saw good results the first few dives, then toxic results, so we discontinued HBOT. Through the years, doctors have readjusted the dive depth for ASD children, and I advise you have yeast eliminated or under control before doing any HBOT therapy. Many families see terrific results in HBOT and helping their children detox.
- **Neurofeedback** This is a type of therapy where your child's brainwaves are monitored during a biofeedback activity. We found this therapy to be helpful with language and focus as we combined behavior and biomedical therapies with neurofeedback. Check your local area for doctors.

## SPIRITUAL REFERENCES

**Tami Duncan-** *LIA Foundation; Autism World Meditations Epiphany Health Arts* www.epiphanyhealingarts.com

**Doreen Virtue** – The Lightworker's Way; Angel Therapy; and Angel Oracle Cards, distributed and published by Hay House Publishing

**Robert Holden** – Shift Happens distributed and published by Hay House Publishing

**Deepak Chopra** – *Creating Abundance Meditation CDs*

## AUTISM REFERENCES

**Genration Rescue-** www.GenerationRescue.org

**TACA- Talk About Curing Autism** - www.tacanow.org

**National Autism Association** – www.nationalautismassociation.org

**Autism Society of America** - www.autism-society.org

Road to Independence; Ready, Set, Potty! by: Brenda Batts

Facing Autism by: Lynn M. Hamilton is a resource book for identifying autism and treatments.

***Talking in Videos…an Autism Language*** – On line video series based on Jonathan and his ability to translate video titles & meanings into everyday langue to build his communication. www.MyAutismHatRack.com

# Notes

Maureen Brice Bordelon is a native Dallasite: born and bred. She met her loving hubby David, another native Dallasite, at the Original Ice House on Knox Street and three years later decided to make the match legal. 23 years of marriage (and counting), 3 beautiful blessings later, they still reside in Texas. Every day is met with laughter, love & gratitude while wearing many "Hats".

For more "Hats" go to www.MyAutismHatRack.com

To learn how to "decode" your child's scripting video language go to www.MyAutismHatRack.com and purchase
*Talking in Videos…an Autism Language*

You can follow Maureen and the continuing journey on twitter @MyAutismHatRack and Facebook at My Autism HatRack

www.ingramcontent.com/pod-product-compliance
Lightning Source LLC
Chambersburg PA
CBHW032120090426
42743CB00007B/406